interchange

FIFTH EDITION

1

Student's Book

Jack C. Richards
with Jonathan Hull and Susan Proctor

WITH DIGITAL PACK

CAMBRIDGE
UNIVERSITY PRESS

CAMBRIDGE
UNIVERSITY PRESS & ASSESSMENT

Shaftesbury Road, Cambridge CB2 8EA, United Kingdom

One Liberty Plaza, 20th Floor, New York, NY 10006, USA

477 Williamstown Road, Port Melbourne, VIC 3207, Australia

314–321, 3rd Floor, Plot 3, Splendor Forum, Jasola District Centre, New Delhi – 110025, India

103 Penang Road, #05–06/07, Visioncrest Commercial, Singapore 238467

Cambridge University Press & Assessment is a department of the University of Cambridge.

We share the University's mission to contribute to society through the pursuit of education, learning and research at the highest international levels of excellence.

www.cambridge.org
Information on this title: www.cambridge.org/9781009040631

First published 2013
Fifth edition 2017
Fifth edition update published 2021

20 19 18 17 16 15

Printed in Brazil by Forma Certa Grafica Digital LTDA

A catalogue record for this publication is available from the British Library

ISBN 978-1-009-04044-0 Student's Book 1 with eBook
ISBN 978-1-009-04047-1 Student's Book 1A with eBook
ISBN 978-1-009-04048-8 Student's Book 1B with eBook
ISBN 978-1-009-04063-1 Student's Book 1 with Digital Pack
ISBN 978-1-009-04064-8 Student's Book 1A with Digital Pack
ISBN 978-1-009-04065-5 Student's Book 1B with Digital Pack
ISBN 978-1-316-62247-6 Workbook 1
ISBN 978-1-316-62254-4 Workbook 1A
ISBN 978-1-316-62266-7 Workbook 1B
ISBN 978-1-108-40606-2 Teacher's Edition 1
ISBN 978-1-316-62226-1 Class Audio 1
ISBN 978-1-009-04066-2 Full Contact 1 with Digital Pack
ISBN 978-1-009-04067-9 Full Contact 1A with Digital Pack
ISBN 978-1-009-04068-6 Full Contact 1B with Digital Pack
ISBN 978-1-108-40305-4 Presentation Plus Level 1

Additional resources for this publication at www.cambridge.org

Informed by teachers

Teachers from all over the world helped develop *Interchange Fifth Edition.* They looked at everything – from the color of the designs to the topics in the conversations – in order to make sure that this course will work in the classroom.
We heard from 1,500 teachers in:

- Surveys
- Focus Groups
- In-Depth Reviews

We appreciate the help and input from everyone. In particular, we'd like to give the following people our special thanks:

Jader Franceschi, **Actúa Idiomas,** Bento Gonçalves, Rio Grande do Sul, Brazil
Juliana Dos Santos Voltan Costa, **Actus Idiomas,** São Paulo, Brazil
Ella Osorio, **Angelo State University,** San Angelo, TX, US
Mary Hunter, **Angelo State University,** San Angelo, TX, US
Mario César González, **Angloamericano de Monterrey, SC,** Monterrey, Mexico
Samantha Shipman, **Auburn High School,** Auburn, AL, US
Linda, **Bernick Language School,** Radford, VA, US
Dave Lowrance, **Bethesda University of California,** Yorba Linda, CA, US
Tajbakhsh Hosseini, **Bezmialem Vakif University,** Istanbul, Turkey
Dilek Gercek, **Bil English,** Izmir, Turkey
erkan kolat, **Biruni University, ELT,** Istanbul, Turkey
Nika Gutkowska, **Bluedata International,** New York, NY, US
Daniel Alcocer Gómez, **Cecati 92,** Guadalupe, Nuevo León, Mexico
Samantha Webb, **Central Middle School,** Milton-Freewater, OR, US
Verónica Salgado, **Centro Anglo Americano,** Cuernavaca, Mexico
Ana Rivadeneira Martínez and Georgia P. de Machuca, **Centro de Educación Continua – Universidad Politécnica del Ecuador,** Quito, Ecuador
Anderson Francisco Guimerães Maia, **Centro Cultural Brasil Estados Unidos,** Belém, Brazil
Rosana Mariano, **Centro Paula Souza,** São Paulo, Brazil
Carlos de la Paz Arroyo, Teresa Noemí Parra Alarcón, Gilberto
Bastida Gaytan, Manuel Esquivel Román, and Rosa Cepeda Tapia, **Centro Universitario Angloamericano,** Cuernavaca, Morelos, Mexico
Antonio Almeida, **CETEC,** Morelos, Mexico
Cinthia Ferreira, **Cinthia Ferreira Languages Services,** Toronto, ON, Canada
Phil Thomas and Sérgio Sanchez, **CLS Canadian Language School,** São Paulo, Brazil
Celia Concannon, **Cochise College,** Nogales, AZ, US
Maria do Carmo Rocha and CAOP English team, **Colégio Arquidiocesano Ouro Preto – Unidade Cônego Paulo Dilascio,** Ouro Preto, Brazil
Kim Rodriguez, **College of Charleston North,** Charleston, SC, US
Jesús Leza Alvarado, **Coparmex English Institute,** Monterrey, Mexico
John Partain, **Cortazar,** Guanajuato, Mexico
Alexander Palencia Navas, **Cursos de Lenguas, Universidad del Atlántico,** Barranquilla, Colombia
Kenneth Johan Gerardo Steenhuisen Cera, Melfi Osvaldo Guzman Triana, and Carlos Alberto Algarín Jiminez, **Cursos de Lenguas Extranjeras Universidad del Atlantico,** Barranquilla, Colombia
Jane P Kerford, **East Los Angeles College,** Pasadena, CA, US
Daniela, **East Village,** Campinas, São Paulo
Rosalva Camacho Orduño, **Easy English for Groups S.A. de C.V.,** Monterrey, Nuevo León, Mexico
Adonis Gimenez Fusetti, **Easy Way Idiomas,** Ibiúna, Brazil
Eileen Thompson, **Edison Community College,** Piqua, OH, US
Ahminne Handeri O.L Froede, **Englishouse escola de idiomas,** Teófilo Otoni, Brazil
Ana Luz Delgado-Izazola, **Escuela Nacional Preparatoria 5, UNAM,** Mexico City, Mexico
Nancy Alarcón Mendoza, **Facultad de Estudios Superiores Zaragoza, UNAM,** Mexico City, Mexico
Marcilio N. Barros, **Fast English USA,** Campinas, São Paulo, Brazil
Greta Douthat, **FCI Ashland,** Ashland, KY, US
Carlos Lizárraga González, **Grupo Educativo Anglo Americano, S.C.,** Mexico City, Mexico
Hugo Fernando Alcántar Valle, **Instituto Politécnico Nacional, Escuela Superior de Comercio y Administración-Unidad Santotomás, Celex Esca Santo Tomás,** Mexico City, Mexico
Sueli Nascimento, **Instituto Superior de Educação do Rio de Janeiro,** Rio de Janeiro, Brazil
Elsa F Monteverde, **International Academic Services,** Miami, FL, US
Laura Anand, **Irvine Adult School,** Irvine, CA, US
Prof. Marli T. Fernandes (principal) and Prof. Dr. Jefferson J. Fernandes (pedagogue), **Jefferson Idiomass,** São Paulo, Brazil
Herman Bartelen, **Kanda Gaigo Gakuin,** Tokyo, Japan
Cassia Silva, **Key Languages,** Key Biscayne, FL, US
Sister Mary Hope, **Kyoto Notre Dame Joshi Gakuin,** Kyoto, Japan
Nate Freedman, **LAL Language Centres,** Boston, MA, US
Richard Janzen, **Langley Secondary School,** Abbotsford, BC, Canada

Christina Abel Gabardo, **Language House,** Campo Largo, Brazil
Ivonne Castro, **Learn English International,** Cali, Colombia
Julio Cesar Maciel Rodrigues, **Liberty Centro de Línguas,** São Paulo, Brazil
Ann Gibson, **Maynard High School,** Maynard, MA, US
Martin Darling, **Meiji Gakuin Daigaku,** Tokyo, Japan
Dax Thomas, **Meiji Gakuin Daigaku,** Yokohama, Kanagawa, Japan
Derya Budak, **Mevlana University,** Konya, Turkey
B Sullivan, **Miami Valley Career Technical Center International Program,** Dayton, OH, US
Julio Velazquez, **Milo Language Center,** Weston, FL, US
Daiane Siqueira da Silva, Luiz Carlos Buontempo, Marlete Avelina de Oliveira Cunha, Marcos Paulo Segatti, Morgana Eveline de Oliveira, Nadia Lia Gino Alo, and Paul Hyde Budgen, **New Interchange-Escola de Idiomas,** São Paulo, Brazil
Patrícia França Furtado da Costa, Juiz de Fora, Brazil
Patricia Servín
Chris Pollard, **North West Regional College SK,** North Battleford, SK, Canada
Olga Amy, **Notre Dame High School,** Red Deer, Canada
Amy Garrett, **Ouachita Baptist University,** Arkadelphia, AR, US
Mervin Curry, **Palm Beach State College,** Boca Raton, FL, US
Julie Barros, **Quality English Studio,** Guarulhos, São Paulo, Brazil
Teodoro González Saldaña and Jesús Monserrrta Mata Franco, **Race Idiomas,** Mexico City, Mexico
Autumn Westphal and Noga La`or, **Rennert International,** New York, NY, US
Antonio Gallo and Javy Palau, **Rigby Idiomas,** Monterrey, Mexico Tatiane Gabriela Sperb do Nascimento, **Right Way,** Igrejinha, Brazil
Mustafa Akgül, **Selahaddin Eyyubi Universitesi,** Diyarbakır, Turkey
James Drury M. Fonseca, **Senac Idiomas Fortaleza,** Fortaleza, Ceara, Brazil
Manoel Fialho S Neto, **Senac – PE,** Recife, Brazil
Jane Imber, **Small World,** Lawrence, KS, US
Tony Torres, **South Texas College,** McAllen, TX, US
Janet Rose, **Tennessee Foreign Language Institute,** College Grove, TN, US
Todd Enslen, **Tohoku University,** Sendai, Miyagi, Japan
Daniel Murray, **Torrance Adult School,** Torrance, CA, US
Juan Manuel Pulido Mendoza, **Universidad del Atlántico,** Barranquilla, Colombia
Juan Carlos Vargas Millán, **Universidad Libre Seccional Cali,** Cali (Valle del Cauca), Colombia
Carmen Cecilia Llanos Ospina, **Universidad Libre Seccional Cali,** Cali, Colombia
Jorge Noriega Zenteno, **Universidad Politécnica del Valle de México,** Estado de México, Mexico
Aimee Natasha Holguin S., **Universidad Politécnica del Valle de México UPVM,** Tultitlàn Estado de México, Mexico
Christian Selene Bernal Barraza, **UPVM Universidad Politécnica del Valle de México,** Ecatepec, Mexico
Lizeth Ramos Acosta**, Universidad Santiago de Cali,** Cali, Colombia
Silvana Dushku, **University of Illinois Champaign,** IL, US
Deirdre McMurtry, **University of Nebraska – Omaha,** Omaha, NE, US
Jason E Mower, **University of Utah,** Salt Lake City, UT, US
Paul Chugg, **Vanguard Taylor Language Institute,** Edmonton, Alberta, Canada
Henry Mulak, **Varsity Tutors,** Los Angeles, CA, US
Shirlei Strucker Calgaro and Hugo Guilherme Karrer, **VIP Centro de Idiomas,** Panambi, Rio Grande do Sul, Brazil
Eleanor Kelly, **Waseda Daigaku Extension Centre,** Tokyo, Japan
Sherry Ashworth, **Wichita State University,** Wichita, KS, US
Laine Bourdene, **William Carey University,** Hattiesburg, MS, US
Serap Aydın, Istanbul, Turkey
Liliana Covino, Guarulhos, Brazil
Yannuarys Jiménez, Barranquilla, Colombia
Juliana Morais Pazzini, Toronto, ON, Canada
Marlon Sanches, Montreal, Canada

Additional content contributed by Kenna Bourke, Inara Couto, Nic Harris, Greg Manin, Ashleigh Martinez, Laura McKenzie, Paul McIntyre, Clara Prado, Lynne Robertson, Mari Vargo, Theo Walker, and Maria Lucia Zaorob.

Classroom Language Student questions

Plan of Book 1

Pronunciation/Listening	Writing/Reading	Interchange Activity
Linked sounds Listening for names, countries, and school subjects	Writing questions requesting personal information "Is Your Name Trendy?": Reading about popular names	"Getting to know you": Collecting personal information about classmates PAGE 114
Syllable stress Listening to descriptions of jobs and daily routines	Writing a biography of a classmate "My Parents Don't Understand My Job!": Reading about four jobs	"What we have in common": Finding similarities in classmates' daily schedules PAGE 115
Sentence stress Listening to people shopping; listening for items, colors, and prices	Writing about favorite clothes "Online Shopping: The Crazy Things People Buy": Reading about unusual online items	"Flea market": Buying and selling things PAGES 116–117
Intonation in questions Listening for likes and dislikes	Writing text messages "The World's Most Powerful Female Musician": Reading about a famous musician	"Are you free this weekend?": Making plans; inviting and giving excuses PAGE 118
Intonation in statements Listening for family relationships	Writing an email about family "Do Families Spend a Lot of Time Together?": Reading about four families	"Is that true?": Finding out information about classmates' families PAGE 119
Intonation with direct address Listening to people talking about free-time activities; listening to descriptions of sports participation	Writing about weekly activities "Fit and Healthy? Take the Quiz!": Reading about health and taking a quiz	"What's your talent?": Finding out about classmates' abilities PAGE 120
Reduction of *did you* Listening to descriptions and opinions of past events and vacations	Writing a blog post "Awesome Vacations": Reading about different kinds of vacations	"Memories": Playing a board game PAGE 121
Reduction of *there is/there are* Listening for locations and descriptions of places	Writing about neighborhoods "Hip Neighborhoods of the World": Reading about popular neighborhoods	"Where are we?": describing and guessing locations PAGE 122

Pronunciation/Listening	Writing/Reading	Interchange Activity
Contrastive stress Listening to descriptions of people; identifying people	Writing an email describing a person "The Age of Selfies": Reading about the history of selfies	"Find the differences": Comparing two pictures of a party **PAGES 123–124**
Linked sounds Listening to descriptions of events	Writing an email to an old friend "Unique Experiences": Reading about four peoples' unusual experiences	"Fun survey": Finding out about a classmate's lifestyle **PAGE 125**
Can't and *shouldn't* Listening to descriptions of cities, towns, and countries	Writing about hometowns "A Big 'Hello!' From . . . ": Reading about interesting cities	"Welcome to our city!": Creating a guide to fun places in a city **PAGE 126**
Reduction of *to* Listening to health problems and advice	Writing a blog post "Toothache? Visit the Rain Forest!": Reading about a plant used as medicine	"What should I do?": Give suggestions for situations **PAGE 127**
Stress in responses Listening to restaurant orders	Writing a restaurant review "To Tip or Not to Tip?": Reading about tipping customs	"Planning a food festival": Creating a menu **PAGE 128**
Questions of choice Listening to a TV quiz show	Writing an article about a place "Earth's Cleanest Places": Reading about three very clean places	"How much do you know?": Taking a general knowledge quiz **PAGE 129**
Reduction of *could you* and *would you* Listening to telephone messages	Writing text message requests "Cell Phone Trouble!": Reading about cell phone problems	"Weekend plans": Finding out about classmates' weekend plans **PAGE 130**
Vowel sounds /oʊ/ and /ʌ/ Listening to descriptions of changes	Writing a plan for a class trip "A Goal Accomplished": Reading about a person's goals	"Our possible future": Planning a possible future **PAGE 131**

1 Where are you from?

- Introduce oneself and others
- Talk about oneself and learn about others

1 CONVERSATION Please call me Alexa.

Listen and practice.

Arturo: Hello, I'm Arturo Valdez.
Alexa: Hi. My name is Alexandra Costa, but please call me Alexa.
Arturo: OK. Where are you from, Alexa?
Alexa: Brazil. How about you?
Arturo: I'm from Mexico.
Alexa: Oh, I love Mexico! It's really beautiful. Oh, good. Soo-jin is here.
Arturo: Who's Soo-jin?
Alexa: She's my classmate. We're in the same business class.
Arturo: Where's she from?
Alexa: South Korea. Let's go and say hello. Sorry, what's your last name again? Vargas?
Arturo: Actually, it's Valdez.
Alexa: How do you spell that?
Arturo: V-A-L-D-E-Z.

2 SPEAKING Checking information

A **PAIR WORK** Introduce yourself with your full name. Use the expressions in the box. Talk to the classmate sitting next to you and to three more classmates.

A: Hi! I'm Akemi Shimizu.
B: I'm sorry. What's your last name again?
A: Shimizu.
B: How do you spell that?

useful expressions

Hi! I'm . . .
I'm sorry. What's your first / last name again?
How do you spell that?
What do people call you?

B **CLASS ACTIVITY** Tell the class the name of the first classmate you talked to. Make a list of names.

"Her name is Akemi Shimizu. She spells her name . . ."

3 CONVERSATION This is Arturo Valdez.

A Listen and practice.

Alexa: Hi Soo-jin, this is Arturo Valdez. He's a biology student.

Soo-jin: Nice to meet you, Arturo. I'm Soo-jin Kim.

Arturo: Hi. So, you're from South Korea?

Soo-jin: That's right. I'm from Seoul.

Arturo: Cool! What's Seoul like?

Soo-jin: It's really nice. It's a very exciting city.

B Listen to the rest of the conversation. What city is Arturo from? What's it like?

4 PRONUNCIATION Linked sounds

Listen and practice. Notice how final consonant sounds are often linked to the vowels that follow them.

I'm a biology student.   My friend is over there.   My name is Alexandra Costa.

5 GRAMMAR FOCUS

Statements with *be*; possessive adjectives

Statements with *be*	Contractions of *be*	Possessive adjectives
I**'m** from Mexico.	I**'m** = I am	my
You**'re** from Brazil.	you**'re** = you are	your
He**'s** from Japan.	he**'s** = he is	his
She**'s** a business student.	she**'s** = she is	her
It**'s** an exciting city.	it**'s** = it is	its
We**'re** in the same class.	we**'re** = we are	our
They**'re** my classmates.	they**'re** = they are	their

GRAMMAR PLUS *see page 132*

A Complete these sentences. Then tell a partner about yourself.

1. ___My___ name is Aiko Yoshida. ______ from Japan. ______ family is in Nagoya. ______ brother is a college student. ______ name is Haruki.
2. ______ name is Matias. ______ from Santiago. ______ a really nice city. ______ sister is a student here. ______ parents are in Chile right now.
3. ______ Angelica, but everyone calls me Angie. ______ last name is Newton. ______ a student at City College. ______ parents are on vacation this week. ______ in Las Vegas.

Wh-questions with *be*

Where's your friend?	He's in class.
Who's Soo-jin?	She's my classmate.
What's Seoul **like**?	It's a very exciting city.
Where are you and Vanessa from?	We're from Brazil.
How are your classes?	They're pretty interesting.
What are your classmates **like**?	They're really nice.

GRAMMAR PLUS *see page 132*

For a list of countries and nationalities, see the appendix at the back of the book.

B Complete these questions. Then practice with a partner.

1. **A:** ___Who's___ that?
   B: Oh, that's Mrs. Adams.
2. **A:** ______________ she from?
   B: She's from San Diego.
3. **A:** ______________ her first name?
   B: It's Caroline.
4. **A:** ______________ the two students over there?
   B: Their names are Mason and Ava.
5. **A:** ______________ they from?
   B: They're from Vancouver.
6. **A:** ______________ they ______________?
   B: They're shy, but very friendly.

C **GROUP WORK** Write five questions about your classmates. Then ask and answer the questions.

What's your last name?
Where's Jay from?

6 SNAPSHOT

SCHOOL SUBJECTS

1 ___math___

2 ______________

3 ______________

4 ______________

5 ______________

6 ______________

7 ______________

8 ______________

Write the names of the school subjects under the pictures.
What is (or was) your favorite school subject?
What subjects don't (or didn't) you like?

math	literature
history	chemistry
physics	geography
biology	physical education

7 CONVERSATION How's it going?

Listen and practice.

Arturo: Hi, Soo-jin!

Soo-jin: Hey Arturo. How's it going?

Arturo: Great! How are you?

Soo-jin: I'm fine, thanks. So, are your classes interesting this semester?

Arturo: Yes, they are. I really love biology.

Soo-jin: Biology? Are you and Alexa in the same class?

Arturo: No, we aren't. My class is in the morning. Her class is in the afternoon.

Soo-jin: Oh, OK. Hey, do you have time for coffee?

Arturo: Sure. I'd love some coffee.

8 GRAMMAR FOCUS

Yes/No questions and short answers with *be*

Are you free?	Yes, I **am**.	No, I**'m not**.
Is Arturo from Mexico?	Yes, he **is**.	No, he**'s not**./No, he **isn't**.
Is Alexa's class in the morning?	Yes, it **is**.	No, it**'s not**./No, it **isn't**.
Are you and Alexa in the same class?	Yes, we **are**.	No, we**'re not**./No, we **aren't**.
Are your classes interesting?	Yes, they **are**.	No, they**'re not**./No, they **aren't**.

GRAMMAR PLUS *see page 132*

A Complete the conversations. Then practice with a partner.

1. **A:** __Is__ Mr. Jones from the United States?
   B: Yes, he ________. ________ from Baltimore.
2. **A:** ________ English class at 2:00?
   B: No, it ________. ________ at 3:00.
3. **A:** ________ you and Giovanna from Italy?
   B: Yes, we ________. ________ from Milan.
4. **A:** ________ Mr. and Mrs. Flores Brazilian?
   B: No, they ________. ________ Peruvian.

B Answer these questions. If you answer "no," give the correct information. Then ask your partner the questions.

1. Are you from the United States? ________________
2. Is your teacher from Canada? ________________
3. Is your English class in the morning? ________________
4. Are you free after class? ________________

C **GROUP WORK** Write five questions about your classmates. Then ask and answer the questions.

Are Kate and Phil from Chicago?

9 WORD POWER Hello and good-bye

A Do you know these expressions? Which ones are "hellos" and which ones are "good-byes"? Complete the chart. Add expressions of your own.

✓ Bye.	How are you?
✓ Good morning.	How's it going?
Good night.	See you later.
Have a good day.	See you tomorrow.
Hey.	Talk to you later.
Hi.	What's up?

Hello	Good-bye
Good morning.	*Bye.*

B Match each expression with the best response.

1. Have a good day.	**a.** Oh, not much.
2. Hi. How are you?	**b.** Thank you. You, too.
3. What's up?	**c.** Good morning.
4. Good morning.	**d.** Pretty good, thanks.

C **CLASS ACTIVITY** Practice saying hello. Then practice saying good-bye.

A: Hi, Sakura. How's it going?
B: Pretty good, thanks. How are you?

10 LISTENING Everyone calls me Bill.

Listen to the conversations. Complete the information about each person.

First name	Last name	Where from?	What do they study?
1. *William*			
2.	*Ortiz*		
3. *Min-soo*			

11 INTERCHANGE 1 Getting to know you

Find out about your classmates. Go to Interchange 1 on page 114.

12 READING

A Look at the names in the article. Are any of the names popular in your country? What similar names can you think of?

IS YOUR NAME *Trendy?*

Some people have names that are very unusual and unique. Think about the actress Emily Blunt, for example. Her daughters' names are Hazel (an eye color) and Violet (a flower). Alicia Keys has a son named Egypt. How cool is that? Are these names trendy? The answer is . . . maybe.

Many names seem to be trendy for a while, just like clothes. In the United States, some grandmothers and great-grandmothers have names like Mildred and Dorothy. For grandfathers and great-grandfathers, it's old names like Eugene or Larry. These names usually come from Greek and Latin, but they're not very popular now.

Parents sometimes choose names because they like an actor or a famous person. That's how trends usually start. For example, David and Victoria Beckham have a son named Brooklyn and a daughter named Harper. Now, Brooklyn is a popular boy's name and Harper is a popular girl's name. In the United Kingdom, baby boys often get the name George because of Prince George, Prince William and Kate Middleton's first child.

There is also a trend for names that are things or places (like Egypt). Flower names are becoming more popular: Poppy, Daisy, and Lotus, for example. Space names are cool, too. More and more babies have names like Orion (a star), Luna (the moon), or Mars (a planet).

POPULAR NAMES FOR BOYS & GIRLS

Can you guess who helped make these names popular?

BOYS	GIRLS
Bruno	January
Leonardo	Angelina
Liam	Audrey

Bruno Mars, Leonardo di Caprio, Liam Hemsworth, January Jones, Angelina Jolie, Audrey Hepburn

B Read the article. Then check (✓) the sentences that are true.

- ☐ **1.** Baby names like Mildred and Larry aren't so trendy now.
- ☐ **2.** Many babies are named after clothes.
- ☐ **3.** Alicia Keys has a son named Hazel.
- ☐ **4.** There is a famous prince named George.
- ☐ **5.** Some girls' names are the same as flower names.
- ☐ **6.** Babies never have names that are the same as planets or stars.

C **GROUP WORK** What names do you like? Can you think of anyone with an unusual name? Do you know how they got that name? Tell your classmates.

2 What do you do?

- ▸ Ask and answer questions about jobs
- ▸ Describe routines and daily schedules

1 SNAPSHOT

Six Popular Part-time Jobs in the United States

Which jobs are easy? difficult? exciting? boring? Why?
Are these good jobs for students? What are some other part-time jobs?

2 WORD POWER Jobs

A Complete the word map with jobs from the list.

- ✓ accountant
- ✓ cashier
- chef
- ✓ dancer
- ✓ flight attendant
- musician
- pilot
- receptionist
- server
- singer
- tour guide
- web designer

JOBS

OFFICE WORK	FOOD SERVICE	TRAVEL INDUSTRY	ENTERTAINMENT BUSINESS
accountant	*cashier*	*flight attendant*	*dancer*
______	______	______	______
______	______	______	______
______	______	______	______
______	______	______	______

B Add two more jobs to each category. Then compare with a partner.

3 SPEAKING Work and workplaces

GROUP WORK Form teams. One team member sits with his or her back to the board. Choose a job from page 8 or from the box. Write the job on the board. Your team member asks yes/no questions and tries to guess the job.

More jobs	
carpenter	nurse
cook	office manager
dentist	police officer
doctor	reporter
engineer	restaurant host
firefighter	salesperson
front desk clerk	security guard
graphic designer	taxi driver
lawyer	teacher
mechanic	vendor

A: Does the person work in a hospital?
B: No, he or she doesn't.
A: Does he or she work in a restaurant?
C: Yes, that's right!

4 CONVERSATION I'm on my feet all day.

A Listen and practice.

Amy: What do you do, Derek?
Derek: I work part-time as a server.
Amy: Oh, really? What restaurant do you work at?
Derek: I work at Stella's Café downtown.
Amy: That's cool. How do you like it?
Derek: It's OK. I'm on my feet all day, so I'm always tired. What do you do?
Amy: I'm a dancer.
Derek: A dancer! How exciting!
Amy: Yeah, it's great! I work with incredible people.
Derek: That sounds really nice. But is it difficult?
Amy: A little. I'm on my feet all day, too, but I love it.

B Listen to the rest of the conversation. Who does Amy travel with? Who does she meet in other cities?

5 GRAMMAR FOCUS

Simple present Wh-questions and statements

		I/You	He/She
What do you **do**?	**I'm** a student. I **have** a part-time job, too.	work	works
Where do you **work**?	I **work** at a restaurant.	take	takes
Where do you **go** to school?	I **go** to the University of Texas.	study	studies
What does Amy **do**?	She**'s** a dancer.	teach	teaches
Where does she **work**?	She **works** at a dance company. She **travels**, too.	do	does
		go	goes
How does she **like** it?	She **loves** it.	have	has

GRAMMAR PLUS *see page 133*

A Complete these conversations. Then practice with a partner.

1. **A:** What ___*do*___ you ___*do*___?
   B: I'm a full-time student. I study the piano.
   A: And ______________ do you ______________ to school?
   B: I ______________ to the Brooklyn School of Music.
   A: Wow! ______________ do you like your classes?
   B: I ______________ them a lot.
2. **A:** What ______________ Tanya do?
   B: She's a teacher. She ______________ an art class at a school in Denver.
   A: And what about Ryan? Where ______________ he work?
   B: He ______________ for a big computer company in San Francisco.
   A: ______________ does he do, exactly?
   B: He's a web designer. He ______________ fantastic websites.
3. **A:** What ______________ Bruce and Ivy do?
   B: They ______________ at an Italian restaurant. It's really good.
   A: That's nice. ______________ is Ivy's job?
   B: Well, she manages the finances and Bruce ______________ in the kitchen.
4. **A:** Where ______________ Ali work?
   B: He ______________ at the university. He ______________ a part-time job.
   A: Really? What ______________ he do?
   B: He ______________ office work.
   A: How ______________ he like it?
   B: Not much, but he ______________ some extra money to spend!

B **PAIR WORK** Ask your partner questions like these about work and school. Take notes to use in Exercise 6.

What do you do?
Do you go to school or do you have a job?
How do you like . . . ?
Do you study another language?
What's your favorite . . . ?
What does your best friend do?

C **CLASS WORK** Tell the class about your partner.

"Regina goes to Chicago University, and she has a part-time job, too. She likes . . ."

6 WRITING A biography

A Use your notes from Exercise 5 to write a biography of your partner. Don't use your partner's name. Use *he* or *she* instead.

> My partner is a chef. She works in a very nice restaurant near our school. She cooks Italian food and bakes desserts. She likes her English classes a lot. Her favorite activities are speaking and vocabulary practice. She studies another language, too . . .

B **CLASS ACTIVITY** Pass your biographies around the class. Guess who each biography is about.

7 CONVERSATION I work in the afternoon.

A Listen and practice.

KRISTINA I need to go to National Bank downtown, please. I'm late for a meeting.

TAXI DRIVER No problem. What time is your meeting?

KRISTINA In 10 minutes! I don't usually work in the morning.

TAXI DRIVER Really? What time do you usually go to work?

KRISTINA I work in the afternoon. I start at one.

TAXI DRIVER That's pretty late. Do you like to work in the afternoon?

KRISTINA Yes, I do. I work better in the afternoon. I finish at seven or eight, then I go home and eat dinner at around 10:30.

TAXI DRIVER Wow, you have dinner late! I go to bed every night at 8:00.

KRISTINA Really? That seems so early!

B Listen to the rest of the conversation. What time does the taxi driver start work? What time does he finish?

8 PRONUNCIATION Syllable stress

A Listen and practice. Notice which syllable has the main stress.

● •	● • •	• ● •
dancer	salesperson	accountant
______	______	______
______	______	______

B Which stress pattern do these words have? Add them to the columns in part A. Then listen and check.

carpenter musician firefighter reporter server tutor

9 GRAMMAR FOCUS

Time expressions

				Expressing clock time
I get up	**at** 7:00	**in** the morning	**on** weekdays.	7:00
I leave work	**early**	**in** the afternoon	**on** Thursdays.	seven
I go to bed	**around** eleven	**in** the evening	**on** weeknights.	seven o'clock
I get home	**late**	**at** night	**on** weekends.	7:00 A.M. = 7:00 in the morning
I stay up	**until** midnight	**on** Fridays.		7:00 P.M. = 7:00 in the evening
I exercise	**before** noon	**on** Saturdays.		
I wake up	**after** noon	**on** Sundays.		

GRAMMAR PLUS *see page 133*

A Choose the correct word.

1. I get up (**at**) / **until** six **at** / **on** weekdays.
2. I have lunch **at** / **early** 11:30 **in** / **on** Mondays.
3. I have a snack **in** / **around** 10:00 **in** / **at** night.
4. **In** / **On** Fridays, I leave school **early** / **before**.
5. I stay up **before** / **until** 1:00 A.M. **in** / **on** weekends.
6. I sleep **around** / **until** noon **in** / **on** Sundays.
7. I have dinner **at** / **in** 7:00 **at** / **on** weeknights.
8. I read a book **after** / **before** I go to sleep.
9. **In** / **On** weekends, I go to bed **in** / **at** 1:00 A.M.
10. **In** / **On** Thursdays, I leave work **at** / **in** 9:00 P.M.
11. I work **late** / **until** on Wednesdays.
12. I study **around** / **until** 11:00 **after** / **early** dinner.

B Rewrite the sentences in part A so that they are true for you. Then compare with a partner.

C **PAIR WORK** Take turns asking and answering these questions.

1. Which days do you get up early? late?
2. What's something you do in the morning?
3. What's something you do before English class?
4. What's something you do on Saturday evenings?
5. Which days do you stay up late?
6. Which days do you go to bed early?
7. What do you do after dinner on weeknights?
8. What do you do after lunch on weekends?

10 LISTENING What hours do you work?

A Listen to Aaron, Madison, and Kayla talk about their daily schedules. Complete the chart.

	Aaron	Madison	Kayla
Job	*carpenter*		
Gets up at . . .		*7:00 a.m.*	
Gets home at . . .			
Goes to bed at . . .			

B **CLASS ACTIVITY** Who do you think has the best daily schedule? Why?

11 INTERCHANGE 2 What we have in common

Find out about your classmates' schedules. Go to Interchange 2 on page 115.

12 READING

A Read the title and skim the blog posts. What are these people's jobs? Why do you think their jobs are hard to understand?

MY PARENTS DON'T UNDERSTAND MY JOB!

DANNY BANGKOK, THAILAND

Do you know what a social media manager is? Right, of course you do, but my mom doesn't. Every week, I try to explain my job to her. I work for a company that makes cars. My job is to tell the world how great our cars are. How do I do that? I get up early and write posts for social media. On weekdays, I go online around 7:00 a.m. and sometimes I work until 9:00 at night. The problem is . . . my mom doesn't use social media.

CARLA BUENOS AIRES, ARGENTINA

It's so funny! I explain my job to my dad, but he just looks very confused. I'm a fashion designer. I always get up early on weekdays because I love my job. I have an office, and most days I draw pictures of cool new clothes, like dresses, jeans, and T-shirts. I also go to stores to look at fabrics to use for my clothes. My dad thinks I'm crazy! He just goes to a store and buys stuff to wear. He doesn't know someone has to design it first.

NICO ATHENS, GREECE

So, I'm a sociologist. I study people. Well, I study how people behave. I also study why they behave the way they do. My mom and dad don't understand why I do that. My mom says, "Nico, people are people! They just do normal things!" I don't agree. There are many reasons why people do the things they do, and I love to learn about that.

LISA LOS ANGELES, UNITED STATES

I'm a software engineer, but my dad doesn't know what that means. I tell him that software is the technology inside his computer, his phone, and his tablet. I make apps for smartphones. One app helps people exercise more. It's very cool because it tracks everything you do during the day. You put your phone in your pocket, and the app does the rest. The app tracks your walk to school, your bike ride on the weekend, and more.

B Read the article. Who does the following things? Check (✓) the correct boxes.

Who does something . . .	Danny	Carla	Nico	Lisa
1. . . . to help people get fit?	☐	☐	☐	☐
2. . . . to understand other people?	☐	☐	☐	☐
3. . . . to make things you can wear?	☐	☐	☐	☐
4. . . . to tell other people about their company?	☐	☐	☐	☐

C **PAIR WORK** Which of the four jobs do you think is the most interesting? the most useful? the hardest to explain? What other things are hard to explain? Think about different jobs, hobbies, or classes at school.

Units 1–2 Progress check

SELF-ASSESSMENT

How well can you do these things? Check (✓) the boxes.

I can . . .	Very well	OK	A little
Make an introduction and use basic greeting expressions (Ex. 1)	☐	☐	☐
Show I didn't understand and ask for repetition (Ex. 1)	☐	☐	☐
Ask and answer questions about myself and other people (Ex. 2)	☐	☐	☐
Ask and answer questions about work (Ex. 3, 4)	☐	☐	☐
Ask and answer questions about habits and routines (Ex. 5)	☐	☐	☐

1 ROLE PLAY Introductions

A **PAIR WORK** You are talking to someone at school. Have a conversation. Then change roles and try the role play again.

A: Hi. How are you?
B: . . .
A: By the way, my name is . . .
B: I'm sorry. What's your name again?
A: . . .
B: I'm . . . . Are you a student here?
A: . . . And how about you?
B: . . .
A: Oh, really? And where are you from?

B **GROUP WORK** Join another pair. Introduce your partner.

2 SPEAKING Interview

Write questions for these answers. Then use the questions to interview a classmate.

1. What's ______________________? My name is Midori Oki.
2. ______________________? I'm from Kyoto, Japan.
3. ______________________? Yes, my classes are very interesting.
4. ______________________? My favorite class is English.
5. ______________________? No, my teacher isn't American.
6. ______________________? My classmates are very nice.
7. ______________________? My best friend is Kiara.

3 SPEAKING What a great job!

A What do you know about these jobs? List three things each person does.

software engineer

works on a computer

caregiver

electrician

IT worker

B **GROUP WORK** Compare your lists. Take turns asking about the jobs.

4 LISTENING At Dylan's party

A Listen to Austin and Haley talk about work and school. Complete the chart.

	Austin	Haley
What do you do?		
Where do you work/study?		
How do you like your job/classes?		
What do you do after work/school?		

B **PAIR WORK** Practice the questions in part A. Answer with your own information.

5 SPEAKING Survey: My perfect day

A Imagine your perfect day. Read the questions, then add one more. Then write your answers.

What time do you get up? __________
What do you do after you get up? __________
Where do you go? __________
What do you do in the evening? __________
When do you go to bed? __________
__________ __________

B **PAIR WORK** Talk about your perfect day. Answer any questions.

WHAT'S NEXT?

Look at your Self-assessment again. Do you need to review anything?

3 How much are these?

- ▸ Ask about and describe prices
- ▸ Discuss preferences

1 SNAPSHOT

Which words have a positive meaning? Which have a negative meaning?
What meanings do these colors have for you? What colors do you like to wear?

2 CONVERSATION I'll take it!

A Listen and practice.

SALESCLERK Hi! Can I help you?
CUSTOMER Yes, please. I need a birthday present for my sister.
SALESCLERK That's so nice! What does she like?
CUSTOMER She loves anything blue. How much is this sweater?
SALESCLERK The light blue one? It's $150.
CUSTOMER That's pretty expensive. I love my sister, but I need to eat!
SALESCLERK Well, we have that one, too.
CUSTOMER Which one? The green one?
SALESCLERK Yes, and it's on sale for $28.99.
CUSTOMER Well, she also likes green. I'll take it!

B Listen to the rest of the conversation. What else does the customer look at? Does he buy it?

3 GRAMMAR FOCUS

Demonstratives; *one, ones*

How much is	**this** T-shirt?	**that** T-shirt?	Which **one**?	
	this one?	**that one**?	The blue **one**.	**It's** $28.99.
How much are	**these** sneakers?	**those** sneakers	Which **ones**?	
	these?	**those**?	The gray **ones**.	**They're** $40.

GRAMMAR PLUS *see page 134*

saying prices

99¢ = ninety-nine cents
$28 = twenty-eight dollars
$28.99 = twenty-eight ninety-nine

A Complete these conversations. Then practice with a partner.

1

A: Excuse me. How much are ___those___ jeans?
B: Which ______? Do you mean ______?
A: No, the light blue ______.
B: Oh, ______ are $59.95.
A: Wow! That's expensive!

2

A: How much is ______ backpack?
B: Which ______?
A: The orange ______.
B: It's $36.99. But ______ green ______ is only $22.25.
A: That's not bad. Can I see it, please?

B PAIR WORK Add prices to the items. Then ask and answer questions.

A: How much are these boots?
B: Which ones?
A: The brown ones.
B: They're $95.50.
A: That's expensive!

useful expressions

That's cheap.
That's reasonable.
That's OK/not bad.
That's expensive.

4 PRONUNCIATION Sentence stress

A Listen and practice. Notice that the important words in a sentence have more stress.

● •	• ● •	• • ● •	• • • ●
Let's see . . .	Excuse me.	That's expensive.	Do you mean these?
	I'll take it.	Can I help you?	

B **PAIR WORK** Practice the conversations in Exercise 3, part B again. Pay attention to the sentence stress.

5 ROLE PLAY Can I help you?

A **PAIR WORK** Put items "for sale" on your desk, such as notebooks, watches, phones, or bags.

Student A: You are a salesclerk. Answer the customer's questions.

Student B: You are a customer. Ask the price of each item. Say if you want to buy it.

A: Can I help you?
B: Yes. I like this pen. How much is it?
A: Which one?

B Change roles and try the role play again.

6 LISTENING Wow! It's expensive!

A Listen to two friends shopping. Write the color and price for each item.

	1. tablet	2. headphones	3. sunglasses	4. T-shirt
color				
price				
Do they buy it?	☐ Yes ☐ No	☐ Yes ☐ No	☐ Yes ☐ No	☐ Yes ☐ No

B Listen again. Do they buy the items? Check (✓) Yes or No.

7 INTERCHANGE 3 Flea market

See what kinds of deals you can make as a buyer and a seller.
Go to Interchange 3 on pages 116–117.

8 WORD POWER Materials

A What are these things made of? Label each one. Use the words from the list.

cotton gold leather plastic rubber silk silver wool

1. a ___silk___ tie

2. a __________ bracelet

3. a __________ ring

4. a __________ shirt

5. a __________ belt

6. __________ earrings

7. __________ flip-flops

8. __________ socks

B **PAIR WORK** What other materials are the things in part A sometimes made of? Make a list.

C **CLASS ACTIVITY** Which materials can you find in your classroom?
"Min-hee has gold earrings, and Ray has a leather jacket."

9 CONVERSATION That's a good point.

A Listen and practice.

Alex: I love these dresses! They are perfect for the wedding on Saturday.

Kristin: Yes! I like this black cotton one.

Alex: The black one? Why?

Kristin: It's more stylish for a wedding.

Alex: That's true, but it's the middle of summer. The material of this one is lighter.

Kristin: That's a good point. The wedding is in the afternoon.

Alex: Hmm . . . there's no price tag. Excuse me. How much is this dress?

Clerk: It's $400. Would you like to try it on?

Alex: Oh, no. That's OK. Thanks anyway.

Clerk: You're welcome.

B Listen to the rest of the conversation. What does Alex buy? What does Kristin think of it?

10 GRAMMAR FOCUS

Preferences; comparisons with adjectives

Which dress do you **prefer**?
I **prefer** the blue one. It's **nicer than** the black one.
Which one do you **like more**?
I **like** the blue one **more**. It's **lighter than** the black one.
Which one do you **like better**?
I **like** the black one **better**. It's **more stylish than** the blue one.

Spelling

cheap → cheap**er**
nice → nice**r**
big → big**ger**
pretty → prett**ier**

GRAMMAR PLUS *see page 134*

A Complete these conversations. Then practice with a partner.

1. A: Which of these jackets do you like more?
B: I prefer the leather one. The design is __________ (nice), and it looks __________ (expensive) the wool one.

2. A: These sweaters are nice. Which one do you prefer?
B: I like the gray one better. The color is __________ (pretty). It's __________ (attractive) the brown and orange one.

3. A: Which rings do you like better?
B: I like the silver ones more. They're __________ (small) the gold ones. And they're __________ (cheap).

B **PAIR WORK** Compare the things in part A. Give your own opinions.

A: Which jacket do you like more?
B: I like the wool one better. The color is prettier.

useful expressions

The color is prettier.
The design is nicer.
The style is more attractive.
The material is better.

11 WRITING My favorite clothes

A What do you like to wear? Write about your favorite clothes and compare them to clothes you don't like as much.

My favorite clothes are cotton T-shirts and jeans. T-shirts are more comfortable than shirts and ties, and I think jeans are nicer than pants. I know that suits are more stylish, but . . .

B **GROUP WORK** Take turns reading your descriptions. Ask questions to get more information.

12 READING

A Skim the article. Why do you think people shop online?

Home Posts Archives

ONLINE SHOPPING: The Crazy Things People Buy

In this week's blog, we look at some extraordinary things people can buy online.

1 A PIECE OF THE MOON: $27.50

It's true. You can own a piece of land on the moon. An acre, or about 4,000 square meters, of moon costs $27.50. That's a lot of space for your stuff. In fact, the price of each acre goes down when you buy more land. Imagine what you could do with all that space . . . if you could travel there! But don't worry, you get a certificate that says the land is yours.

2 SOMEONE TO STAND IN LINE FOR YOU: $25 AN HOUR

No one likes to stand in line, right? Now you don't have to! For $25 an hour, someone waits patiently in line to get the stuff you need. Imagine that! Some people pay for someone to stand in line for movie tickets or for a new video game that's on sale. Make a reservation online in just a few clicks.

3 SOME VERY EXPENSIVE SNEAKERS: $20,000 AND UP

Do you ever think your shoes are boring? Well, our sneakers are just what you need. Just go to our online store, look for a pair of sneakers you like, and place a bid. Maybe you'll win! Some of the sneakers are from famous basketball players.

4 NO TIME FOR A REAL PET: $12

Many people like dogs and cats, but they just don't have the time to take care of them. If that sounds like you, here's the answer to your problem: a digital pet rock. It's clean, it's quiet, and it doesn't need food. It comes in a box. We think it's just about the perfect pet. You plug it into your laptop, and it's always with you!

B Read the blog. Find the item and write its name. Then write the number of the paragraph where you find the answers.

Find something . . .

a. . . . that you can wear. ____________________

b. . . . that you use with your laptop. ____________________

c. . . . that saves you a lot of time. ____________________

d. . . . that is huge. ____________________

C **GROUP WORK** The person who invented the first pet rock, Gary Dahl, became a millionaire. Why do you think people bought pet rocks? Do you think Mr. Dahl was a smart man? Would you buy a pet rock? Would you buy any of the other things? How much would you spend? Tell your classmates.

4 Do you play the guitar?

- Discuss entertainment likes and dislikes
- Make, accept, and decline invitations

1 SNAPSHOT

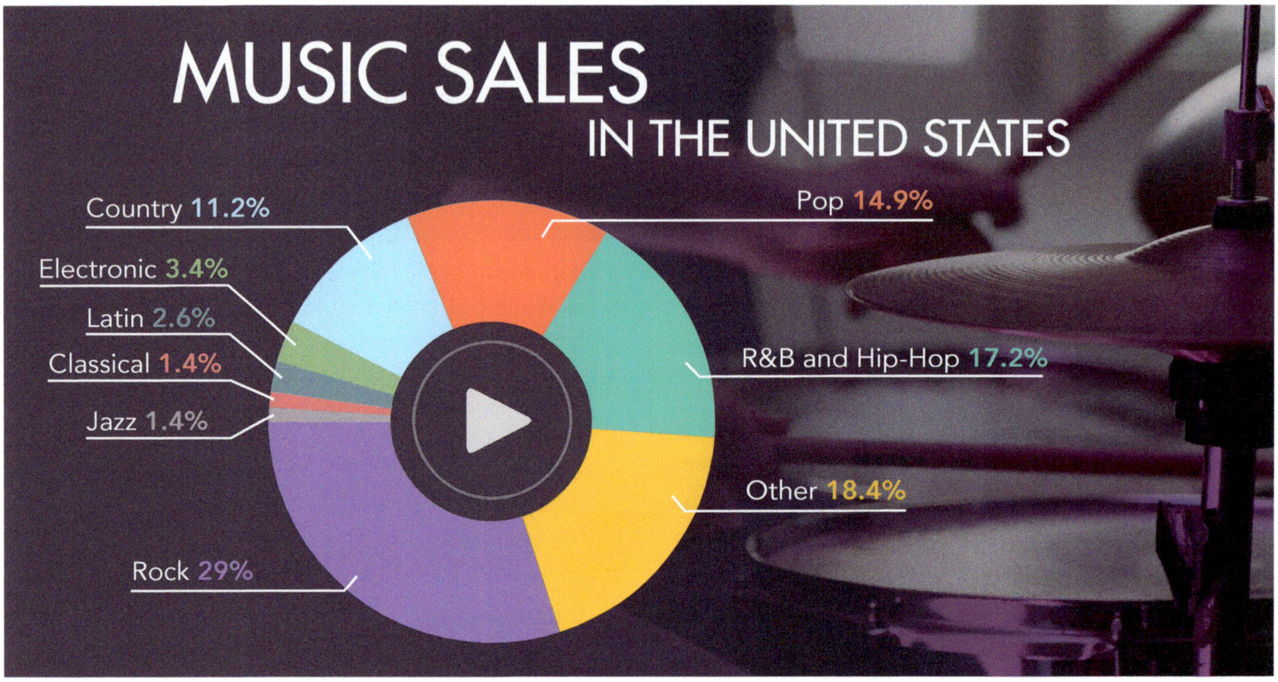

What styles of music do you like? What styles do you dislike?
What styles of music are popular in your country?

2 WORD POWER That's entertainment!

A Complete the word map with words from the list. Some words can go in more than one category.

action	reality show
electronic	reggae
game show	salsa
horror	science fiction
musical	soap opera
rap	talk show

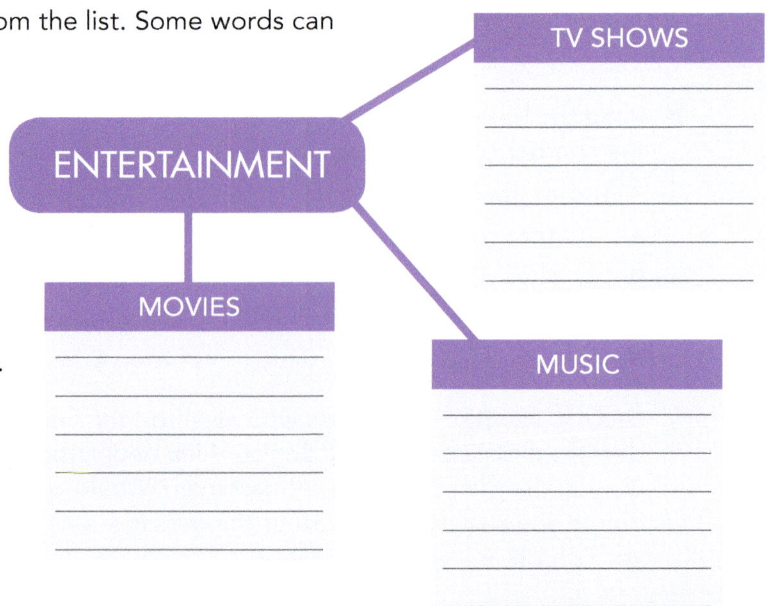

B Add two more words to each category. Then compare with a partner.

C **GROUP WORK** Number the items in each list from 1 (you like it the most) to 6 (you like it the least). Then compare your ideas.

3 CONVERSATION What kind of music do you like?

A Listen and practice.

LEANNE I can't wait for the Taylor Swift concert this Friday!

SETH I think I know her. Does she play the violin?

LEANNE No. She's a pop star.

SETH Of course! I guess I don't listen to pop music a lot.

LEANNE Oh, really? What kind of music do you like?

SETH I really like hip-hop. Drake is my favorite musician.

LEANNE Doesn't Drake play the guitar?

SETH No, Leanne. He sings and raps.

LEANNE OK. Well, I think we need to teach each other about music!

B Listen to the rest of the conversation. Who is Seth's favorite band? Does Leanne like them?

4 GRAMMAR FOCUS

Simple present questions; short answers

Do you **like** country music?
Yes, I **do**. I love it.
No, I **don't**. I don't like it very much.

What kind of music **do** you **like**?
I really like rap.

Does she **play** the piano?
Yes, she **does**. She plays very well.
No, she **doesn't**. She doesn't play an instrument.

What does she **play**?
She plays the guitar.

Do they **like** Imagine Dragons?
Yes, they **do**. They like them a lot.
No, they **don't**. They don't like them at all.

Who do they **like**?
They like Maroon 5.

Object pronouns
me
you
him
her
it
us
them

GRAMMAR PLUS *see page 135*

Complete these conversations. Then practice with a partner.

1. **A:** I like Alabama Shakes a lot. __________ you know __________?
   B: Yes, I __________, and I love this song. Let's download __________.
2. **A:** __________ you like science fiction movies?
   B: Yes, I __________. I like __________ very much.
3. **A:** ______________ Vinnie and Midori like soap operas?
   B: Vinnie __________, but Midori __________. She hates __________.
4. **A:** What kind of music __________ Maya like?
   B: Classical music. She loves Yo-Yo Ma.
   A: Yeah, he's amazing. I like __________ a lot.

Alabama Shakes

5 PRONUNCIATION Intonation in questions

A Listen and practice. Yes/No questions usually have rising intonation. Wh-questions usually have falling intonation.

Do you like pop music?   What kind of music do you like?

B **PAIR WORK** Practice these questions.

Do you like TV?	What shows do you like?
Do you like video games?	What games do you like?
Do you play a musical instrument?	What instrument do you play?

6 SPEAKING Entertainment survey

A **GROUP WORK** Write five questions about entertainment and entertainers. Then ask and answer your questions in groups.

What kinds of . . . do you like?
(music, TV shows, video games)
Do you like . . . ?
(reggae, game shows, action movies)
Who's your favorite . . . ?
(singer, actor, athlete)

B **GROUP WORK** Complete this information about your group. Ask any additional questions.

Our group FAVORITES

What's your favorite kind of . . . ?

music ______________________
movie ______________________
TV show ______________________

What's your favorite . . . ?

song ______________________
movie ______________________
video game ______________________

Who's your favorite . . . ?

singer ______________________
actor ______________________
athlete ______________________

Adele

Steph Curry

Star Wars: The Force Awakens

Top Chef

C **CLASS ACTIVITY** Read your group's list to the class. Find out the class favorites.

7 LISTENING The perfect date

A Listen to a host and four people on a TV game show. Three men want to invite Alexis on a date. What kinds of things do they like? Complete the chart.

	Jacob	Tyler	Andrew	Alexis
Music				
Movies				
TV shows				

B **CLASS ACTIVITY** Who do you think is the best date for Alexis? Why?

8 CONVERSATION What time does it start?

A Listen and practice.

CONNOR I have tickets to my brother's concert on Friday night. Would you like to go?

CAMILA Thanks, I'd love to. What time does it start?

CONNOR At 8:00.

CAMILA Do you want to have dinner before? Maybe at 6:00?

CONNOR Well, I'd like to, but I have to work late. Let's just meet before the concert, around 7:30.

CAMILA No problem. We can have dinner another day. Let's meet at your office and go together.

CONNOR Sounds good! See you on Friday.

B Listen to Connor and Camila talking at the concert. Does Camila like the concert? Does Connor's brother play well?

9 GRAMMAR FOCUS

Would; verb + *to* + verb

Would you **like to go** out on Friday?
Yes, I **would**.
Yes, I'**d love to**. Thanks.

Would you **like to go** to a concert?
I'**d like to**, but I **have to work** late.
I'**d like to**, but I **need to save** money.
I'**d like to**, but I **want to visit** my parents.

Contractions
I'**d** = I would

GRAMMAR PLUS *see page 135*

A Respond to three invitations. Then write three invitations for the given responses.

1. **A:** I have tickets to the soccer game on Sunday. Would you like to go?
   B: ______________________
2. **A:** Would you like to come over for dinner tomorrow night?
   B: ______________________
3. **A:** Would you like to go to a hip-hop dance class with me this weekend?
   B: ______________________
4. **A:** ______________________
   B: Yes, I'd love to. Thank you!
5. **A:** ______________________
   B: Well, I'd like to, but I have to study.
6. **A:** ______________________
   B: Yes, I would. I really like electronic music.

B **PAIR WORK** Ask and answer the questions in part A. Give your own responses.

C **PAIR WORK** Think of three things you would like to do. Then invite a partner to do them with you. Your partner responds and asks follow-up questions like these:

When is it? Where is it? What time does it start? When does it end?

10 WRITING Text messages

A What do these text messages say?

text message abbreviations

u = you	afaik = as far as I know
r = are	lol = laugh out loud
2 = to / too	idk = I don't know
pls = please	msg = message
thx = thanks	nm = never mind
imo = in my opinion	brb = be right back
tbh = to be honest	ttyl = talk to you later

B **GROUP WORK** Write a "text message" to each person in your group. Then exchange messages. Write a response to each message.

11 INTERCHANGE 4 Are you free this weekend?

Make weekend plans with your classmates. Go to Interchange 4 on page 118.

12 READING

A Scan the article and look at the pictures. In what year did each event take place?

The World's Most Powerful FEMALE MUSICIAN

Beyoncé Knowles-Carter is a singer, songwriter, performer, actress, clothing designer, and Grammy Award–winning superstar. Many people call her one of the most powerful female musicians in history. Beyoncé works really hard for her success. As she says, "I wanted to sell a million records, and I sold a million records. I wanted to go platinum; I went platinum. I've been working nonstop since I was 15. I don't even know how to chill out."

Many people talk about Beyoncé's energy on stage. She's an amazing entertainer. Millions of fans love her singing and dancing. Beyoncé uses many different styles of music, including funk, soul, and pop. In her career so far, Beyoncé has sold over 100 million records as a solo artist and another 60 million records with her group Destiny's Child.

BEYONCÉ FAST FACTS

1981	Beyoncé is born in Houston, Texas.
1996	Her girl group, Destiny's Child, gets its first recording contract.
2001	Beyoncé experiences her first time acting. She stars in *Carmen: A Hip Hopera* on MTV.
2003	She releases her first solo album, *Dangerously in Love*.
2004	She wins five Grammys at the Grammy Awards.
2005	Beyoncé starts an organization to help hurricane victims.
2008	She marries rapper Jay-Z.
2010	She wins six Grammys at the Grammy Awards for her album *I Am . . . Sasha Fierce*.
2012	Beyoncé has a daughter and names her Blue Ivy.
2013	Beyoncé performs at the U.S. president's inauguration.
2013	She releases a secret album online named *Beyoncé*.
2016	Beyoncé performs her song "Formation" at a huge sporting event.

Beyoncé marries Jay-Z.

Beyoncé performs at the U.S. president's inauguration.

B Read the article. Then number these sentences from 1 (first event) to 8 (last event).

_____ **a.** She performs at a president's inauguration.
_____ **b.** She is born in Texas.
_____ **c.** She acts in a movie.
_____ **d.** She wins five Grammys.
_____ **e.** She releases her first solo album.
_____ **f.** She has a baby.
_____ **g.** Her group gets its first recording contract.
_____ **h.** She helps hurricane victims.

C **PAIR WORK** Who is your favorite musician? What do you know about his or her life?

Units 3–4 Progress check

SELF-ASSESSMENT

How well can you do these things? Check (✓) the boxes.

I can . . .	Very well	OK	A little
Give and understand information about prices (Ex. 1)	☐	☐	☐
Say what I like and dislike (Ex. 1, 2, 3)	☐	☐	☐
Explain why I like or dislike something (Ex. 2)	☐	☐	☐
Describe and compare objects and possessions (Ex. 2)	☐	☐	☐
Make and respond to invitiations (Ex. 4)	☐	☐	☐

1 LISTENING Price Cut City

A Listen to a commercial for Price Cut City. Choose the correct prices.

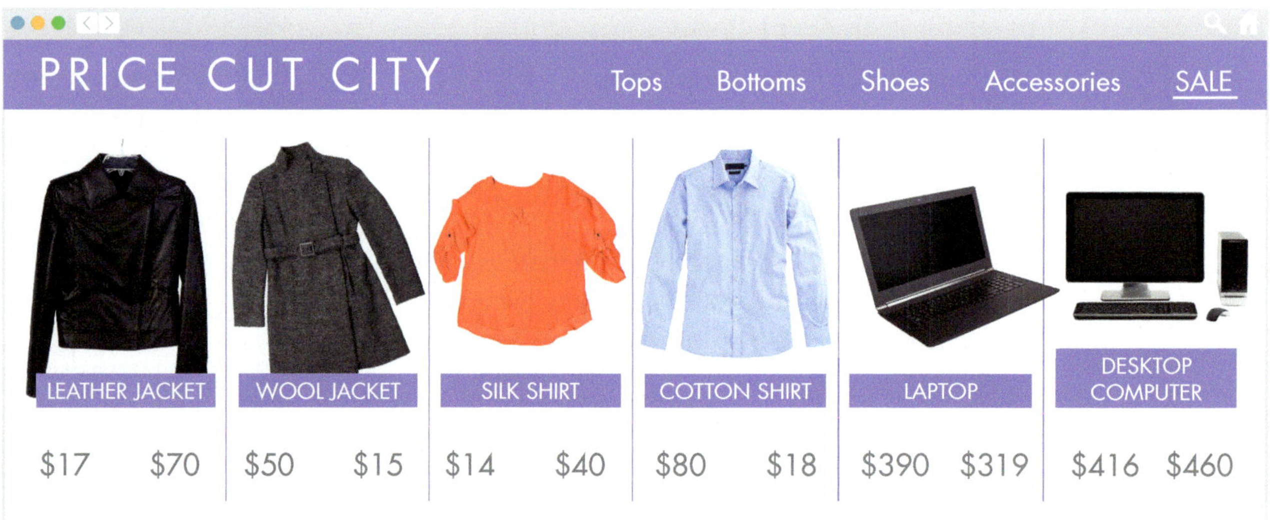

B **PAIR WORK** What do you think of the items in part A? At what stores or websites can you find items like these at low prices? Give your own ideas and opinions.

2 ROLE PLAY Shopping trip

Student A: Choose things from Exercise 1 for your family. Ask for Student B's opinion.
Student B: Help Student A choose presents for his or her family.

> **A:** I want to buy a laptop for my parents. Which one do you like better?
> **B:** Well, I like . . . better. It's nicer, and . . .

Change roles and try the role play again.

3 SPEAKING Survey: Likes and dislikes

A Add one more question to the chart. Write your answers to these questions.

	Me	My classmate
When do you usually watch TV?		
What kinds of TV shows do you like?		
Do you like game shows?		
Do you read the news online?		
Who is your favorite singer?		
What do you think of hip-hop?		
What is your favorite movie?		
Do you like musicals?		
What kinds of movies do you dislike?		
______________		

B **CLASS ACTIVITY** Go around the class. Find someone who has the same answers as you. Write a classmate's name only once!

4 SPEAKING What an excuse!

A Make up three invitations to interesting activities. Write them on cards.

My friends and I are going to the amusement park on Sunday at 2 p.m. Would you like to come?

B Write three response cards. One is an acceptance card, and two are refusals. Think of silly or unusual excuses.

That sounds great! What time do you want to meet?

I'd like to, but I have to wash my cat tomorrow.

I'd love to, but I want to take my bird to a singing contest.

C **GROUP WORK** Shuffle the invitation cards together and the response cards together. Take three cards from each pile. Then invite people to do the things on your invitation cards. Use the response cards to accept or refuse.

WHAT'S NEXT?

Look at your Self-assessment again. Do you need to review anything?

5 What an interesting family!

- Describe families
- Talk about habitual and current activities

1 WORD POWER Family

A Look at Joseph's family tree. How are these people related to him? Add the words to the family tree.

cousin	niece
daughter	sister-in-law
father	uncle
grandmother	wife

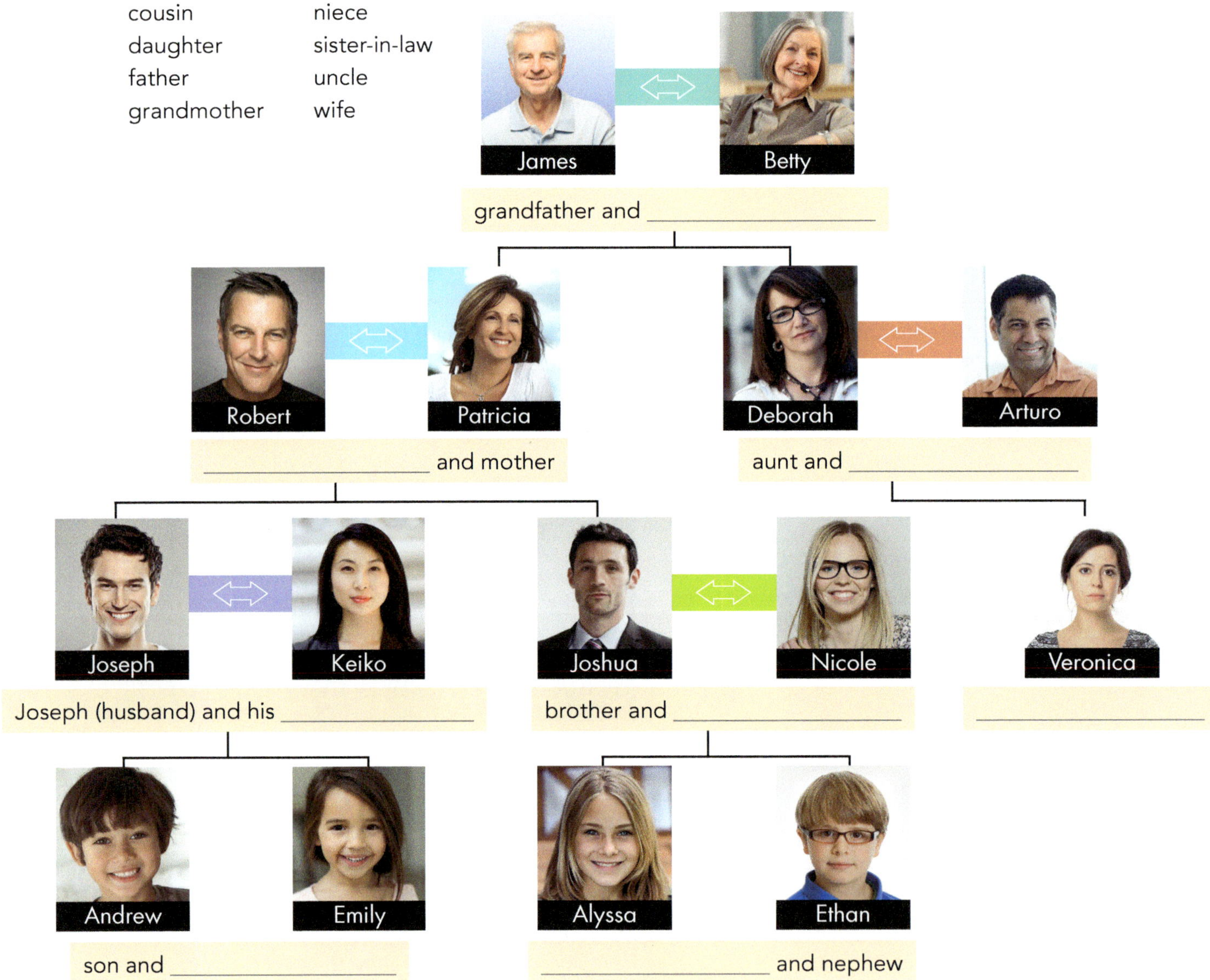

B Draw your family tree (or a friend's family tree). Then take turns talking about your families. Ask follow-up questions to get more information.

A: There are six people in my family. I have one brother and two sisters.

B: How old is your brother?

2 LISTENING Famous relatives

Listen to four conversations about famous people. How is the second person related to the first person?

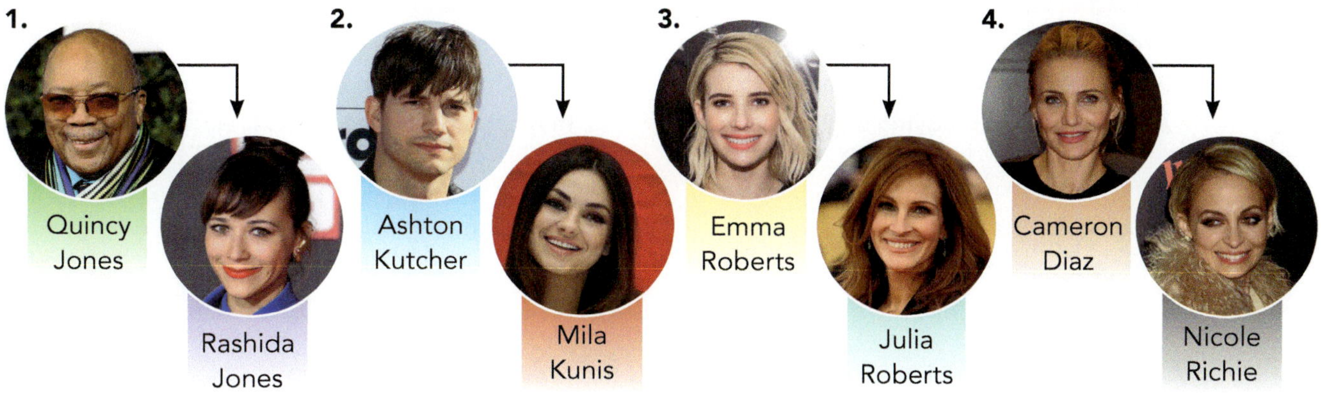

3 CONVERSATION He's traveling in Thailand.

A Listen and practice.

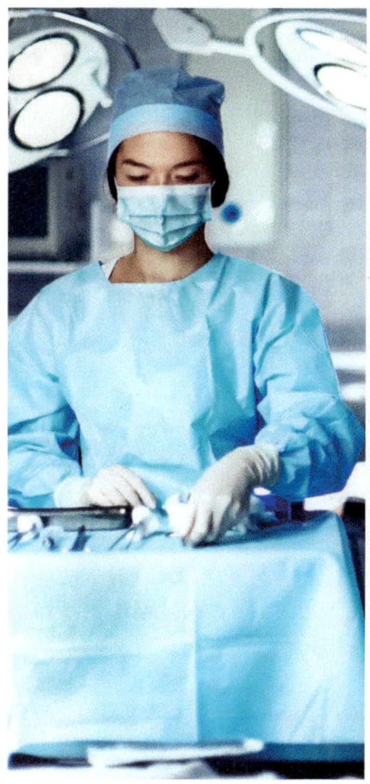

MAX Do you have brothers and sisters, Tina?

TINA Yes, I have a brother and a sister.

MAX Oh, what does your sister do?

TINA She's a surgeon. She works for a medical aid organization.

MAX Wow! And what about your brother?

TINA He's a writer. He travels and writes about his experiences for a magazine.

MAX What an interesting family! Can I meet them?

TINA Sure, but my sister's not here right now. She's treating patients in Cameroon.

MAX And your brother?

TINA He's traveling in Thailand, and then he wants to visit my sister. I miss them!

B Listen to the rest of the conversation. Where do Max's parents live? What do his parents do?

4 PRONUNCIATION Intonation in statements

A Listen and practice. Notice that statements usually have falling intonation.

She's working in Cameroon. He's traveling in Thailand.

B **PAIR WORK** Practice the conversation in Exercise 3 again.

5 GRAMMAR FOCUS

Present continuous

Are you **living** at home now?	Yes, I **am**.	No, I**'m not**.
Is your sister **working** in another city?	Yes, she **is**.	No, she**'s not**./No, she **isn't**.
Are your parents **studying** English this year?	Yes, they **are**.	No, they**'re not**./No, they **aren't**.

Where **are** you **working** now?	I**'m not working**. I need a job.
What **is** your brother **doing**?	He**'s traveling** in Thailand.
What **are** your friends **doing** these days?	They**'re studying** for their exams.

GRAMMAR PLUS *see page 136*

A Complete these phone conversations using the present continuous.

1

A: Hi, Brittany. What ____________ you ____________ (do)?
B: Hey, Zach. I ____________ (eat) a sandwich at O'Connor's.
A: Mmm! Is it good?
B: Yeah. It's delicious. Wait, they ____________ (bring) my dessert now. It's chocolate cake with ice cream. Call you later! Bye!

2

A: So, Madison, how ____________ you and your sister ____________ (do) in college?
B: We ____________ (have) a lot of fun, Mom!
A: Fun? OK, but ____________ your sister ____________ (go) to class every morning?
B: Yeah, Mom. She ____________ (work) hard and I am, too. I'm serious!

B **PAIR WORK** Write a short dialogue using the present continuous, then practice it.

C **CLASS WORK** Read your dialogue to the class.

6 DISCUSSION What are you doing these days?

GROUP WORK Ask and answer questions about what you are doing. Use the topics in the box and your own ideas. Ask follow-up questions to get more information.

A: So, what are you doing these days?
B: I'm playing basketball in college.
A: That's nice. And are you enjoying it?

topics to talk about

traveling	going to high school or college
playing a sport	learning a musical instrument
living alone	working or studying

7 INTERCHANGE 5 Is that true?

Find out about your classmates' families. Go to Interchange 5 on page 119.

8 SNAPSHOT

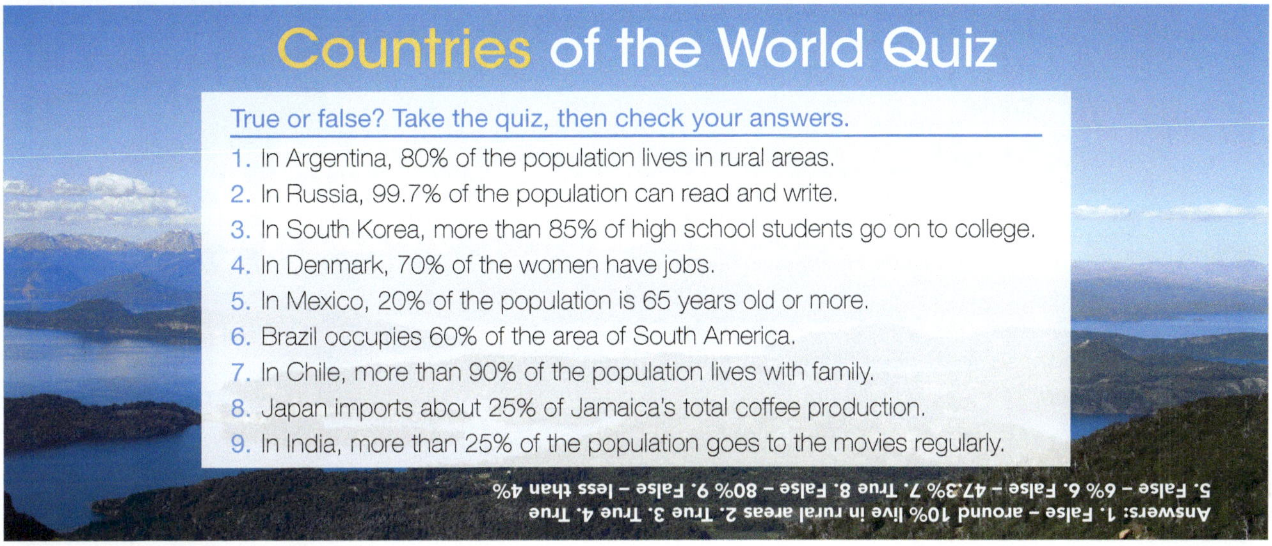

Countries of the World Quiz

True or false? Take the quiz, then check your answers.

1. In Argentina, 80% of the population lives in rural areas.
2. In Russia, 99.7% of the population can read and write.
3. In South Korea, more than 85% of high school students go on to college.
4. In Denmark, 70% of the women have jobs.
5. In Mexico, 20% of the population is 65 years old or more.
6. Brazil occupies 60% of the area of South America.
7. In Chile, more than 90% of the population lives with family.
8. Japan imports about 25% of Jamaica's total coffee production.
9. In India, more than 25% of the population goes to the movies regularly.

Answers: 1. False – around 10% live in rural areas 2. True 3. True 4. True
5. False – 6% 6. False – 47.3% 7. True 8. False – 80% 9. False – less than 4%

Which facts surprise you? Why?
What interesting facts do you know about your country?

9 CONVERSATION I didn't know that.

A Listen and practice.

LUIS What a great picture! Are those your parents?

VICKY Thanks! Yes, it's my favorite picture of us.

LUIS It's really nice. So, do you have any brothers or sisters?

VICKY No, I'm an only child. Actually, a lot of families in China have only one child.

LUIS Oh, really? I didn't know that.

VICKY What about you, Luis?

LUIS I come from a big family. I have two brothers and four sisters.

VICKY Wow! Is that typical in Peru?

LUIS I'm not sure. Many families are smaller these days. But big families are great because you get a lot of birthday presents!

B Listen to the rest of the conversation. What does Vicky like about being an only child?

10 GRAMMAR FOCUS

Quantifiers

100%	**All**	
	Nearly all	families have only one child.
	Most	
	Many	
	A lot of	families are smaller these days.
	Some	
	Not many	couples have more than one child.
	Few	
0%	**No one**	gets married before the age of 18.

GRAMMAR PLUS *see page 136*

A Rewrite these sentences using quantifiers. Then compare with a partner.

1. In the U.S., 69% of high school students go to college.
   ____
2. Seven percent of the people in Brazil are age 65 or older.
   ____
3. In India, 0% of the people vote before the age of 18.
   ____
4. Forty percent of the people in Sweden live alone.
   ____
5. In Canada, 22% of the people speak French at home.
   ____

B PAIR WORK Rewrite the sentences in part A so that they are true about your country.

In the U.S., most high school students go to college.

11 WRITING An email to an online friend

A You have an online friend in another country. Write an email to your friend about your family.

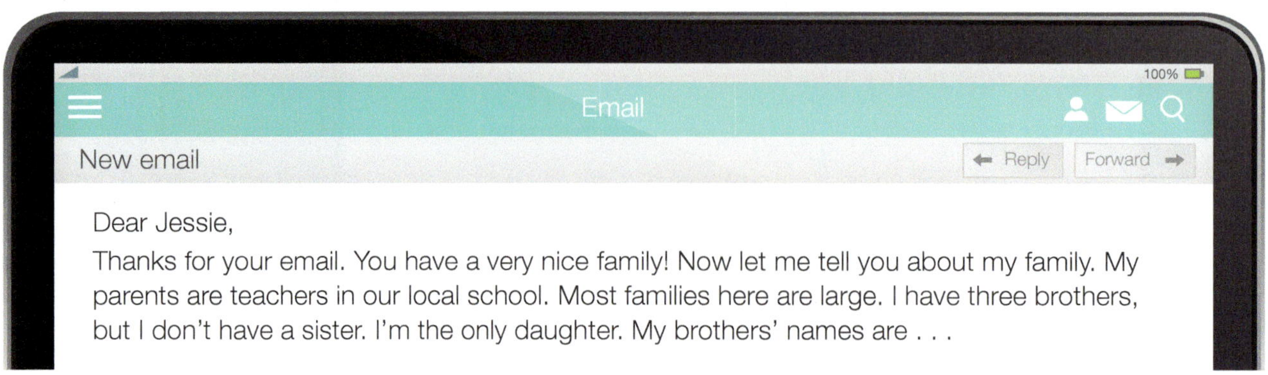

B GROUP WORK Take turns reading your emails. Ask questions to get more information.

12 READING

A A journalist interviewed four people. Read the title of the article. What do you think the answer will be? Check (✓) the answer.

☐ Yes, most families do. ☐ No, most families don't. ☐ Some families do, some families don't.

DO FAMILIES SPEND A LOT OF TIME TOGETHER?

We spend a lot of time together on the weekends. My husband and I always take our son, Oliver, and daughter, Samantha, out to do something fun. Some weeks we go for a long bike ride and get a lot of fresh air! We go to the beach in the summer, of course. In the evenings, we have a barbecue together. During the week, it's more difficult to spend time together because of work and school.

– Jane Chambers

It's a little sad, but most of the time we spend as a family is watching TV. We don't talk much. My mom and dad both work, and they're often tired when they get home. My sister just plays games on her tablet all evening. It's kind of boring. Maybe we spend about an hour a day together. It's never more than that.

– Billy Foster

I'm a stay-at-home dad, and I'm having a great time with my family! When the kids are in school, I do housework. When they come home, I help them with their homework. After that, we all have fun together. We play a lot of sports and read books. I love all the time I get with my two boys.

– Nick Ramos

We're always really busy, but we make an effort to spend time together. My grandparents come over to our house twice a week for dinner. I think family is very important. I often help my mom or dad cook the meals. Sometimes we all go to the movies. I like that a lot.

– Carla Costantini

B Read the interviews. Then check the correct names.

Who . . . ?	**Jane**	**Billy**	**Nick**	**Carla**
1. watches a lot of TV	☐	☐	☐	☐
2. sees their grandparents twice a week	☐	☐	☐	☐
3. spends time outdoors	☐	☐	☐	☐
4. stays at home with the kids	☐	☐	☐	☐
5. doesn't spend much time with family	☐	☐	☐	☐
6. does housework during the day	☐	☐	☐	☐

C **GROUP WORK** What do families look like in your country? Do dads stay at home with their children? Do you think that's a good thing or a bad thing? Is it important to you to spend time with your family?

6 How often do you run?

- Discuss sports and exercise habits
- Ask and answer questions about frequency of free-time activities

1 SNAPSHOT

Top Sports and Fitness Activities in the United States

Sports
- ☐ football
- ☐ baseball
- ☐ soccer
- ☐ ice hockey
- ☐ basketball

Fitness Activities
- ☐ treadmill
- ☐ running/jogging
- ☐ walking
- ☐ bowling
- ☐ weight training

Do people in your country enjoy any of these sports or activities?
Check (✓) the sports or fitness activities you enjoy.
Make a list of other activities you do. Then compare with the class.

2 WORD POWER Sports and fitness

A Which of these activities are popular with the following age groups in your country? Check (✓) the activities. Then compare with a partner.

	Children	Teens	Young adults	Middle-aged people	Older people
bike riding	☐	☐	☐	☐	☐
golf	☐	☐	☐	☐	☐
jogging	☐	☐	☐	☐	☐
martial arts	☐	☐	☐	☐	☐
Pilates	☐	☐	☐	☐	☐
soccer	☐	☐	☐	☐	☐
swimming	☐	☐	☐	☐	☐
volleyball	☐	☐	☐	☐	☐
yoga	☐	☐	☐	☐	☐

B **PAIR WORK** Which activities in part A are used with *do*, *go*, or *play*?

do martial arts	go bike riding	play golf
______	______	______
______	______	______

3 CONVERSATION I run every day.

A Listen and practice.

Aaron: You have a lot of energy, Riley. Do you exercise a lot?
Riley: Well, I get up early and run on the treadmill for an hour every day.
Aaron: Seriously?
Riley: Sure. And I do weight lifting.
Aaron: Wow! How often do you lift weights?
Riley: I usually do it about three times a week. What about you?
Aaron: Oh, I hardly ever exercise. I usually just watch TV or listen to music in my free time. I guess I'm a real couch potato!

B Listen to the rest of the conversation. What else does Riley do in her free time?

4 GRAMMAR FOCUS

Adverbs of frequency

How often do you exercise?	Do you **ever** watch TV in the evening?	100%	**always**
I run on the treadmill **every day**.	Yes, I **often** watch TV after dinner.		**almost always**
I go jogging **once a week**.	I **sometimes** watch TV before bed.		**usually**
I play soccer **twice a month**.	**Sometimes** I watch TV before bed.*		**often**
I swim about **three times a year**.	I **hardly ever** watch TV.		**sometimes**
I don't exercise very **often/much**.	No, I **never** watch TV.		**hardly ever**
Usually I exercise before class.*			**almost never**
		0%	**never**

****Usually** and **sometimes** can begin a sentence.*

GRAMMAR PLUS *see page 137*

A Put the adverbs in the correct place. Sometimes there is more than one correct answer. Then practice with a partner.

1. **A:** Do you play sports? (ever)
   B: Sure. I play soccer. (twice a week)
2. **A:** What do you do on Saturday mornings? (usually)
   B: Nothing much. I sleep until noon. (almost always)
3. **A:** Do you lift weights at the gym? (often)
   B: No, I lift weights. (hardly ever)
4. **A:** Do you exercise on Sundays? (always)
   B: No, I exercise on Sundays. (never)
5. **A:** What do you do after class? (usually)
   B: I go out with my classmates. (about three times a week)
6. **A:** Do you go to the movies? (often)
   B: Yes, I go to the movies. (once a week)
7. **A:** Do you go bike riding? (ever)
   B: No, I ride a bike. (hardly ever)
8. **A:** Do you walk to school? (sometimes)
   B: Sure. I walk to school. (five days a week)

B **PAIR WORK** Take turns asking the questions in part A. Give your own information when answering.

5 PRONUNCIATION Intonation with direct address

A Listen and practice. Notice these statements with direct address. There is usually falling intonation and a pause before the name.

You have a lot of energy, Riley. You look tired, Aaron. I feel great, Dr. Yun.

B **PAIR WORK** Write four statements using direct address. Then practice them.

6 SPEAKING Fitness programs

A **GROUP WORK** Take a poll in your group. Take turns asking each person these questions. Each person gets two points for each *Yes* answer and one point for each *No* answer.

1

Do you have a regular fitness program?

YES ☐ NO ☐

How often do you exercise?

2

Do you ever go to a gym?

YES ☐ NO ☐

How often do you go? What do you do there?

3

Do you play any sports?

YES ☐ NO ☐

Which ones? How often do you play them?

4

Do you ever take long walks?

YES ☐ NO ☐

How often? Where do you go?

5

Do you do anything else to keep fit?

YES ☐ NO ☐

What do you do?

B **GROUP WORK** Add up your points and study the results of the poll. Who in your group got at least six points?

C **CLASS WORK** Tell the class about one of the people in your group.

"Cynthia does Pilates twice a week, and sometimes she goes jogging. She doesn't . . ."

7 LISTENING I swim twice a week.

A Listen to three people discuss what they like to do in the evening. Complete the chart.

	Activity	How often?
Joseph		
Victoria		
Carlos		

B Listen again. Who is most similar to you – Joseph, Victoria, or Carlos?

8 DISCUSSION Olympic sports and athletes

GROUP WORK Take turns asking and answering these questions.

Can you remember the names of five Olympic sports? What are they?
Do you ever watch Olympic sports on TV? Which ones?
Would you like to see Olympic sports live? Why? Why not?
Do you prefer the summer or winter Olympics? Why?
What's your favorite Olympic sport? Why?
What's an Olympic sport that you really don't like? Why not?
Who's a famous male athlete in your country? What sport does he play?
Who's a famous female athlete? What sport does she play?

9 WRITING Your weekly activities

A Write about your weekly activities. Include your favorite activity, but don't say which one is your favorite.

I usually exercise four or five times a week. I always do yoga on Mondays and Wednesdays. I often go jogging in the morning on Tuesdays and Thursdays. I sometimes go to the beach and play volleyball with my friends on weekends. I . . .

B **GROUP WORK** Take turns reading your descriptions. Can you guess your partners' favorite activities?

"Your favorite activity is volleyball, right?"

10 CONVERSATION You're in great shape.

A Listen and practice.

STEPH You're in great shape, Mick.
MICK Thanks. I guess I'm a real fitness freak.
STEPH How often do you work out?
MICK Well, I go swimming and lift weights every day. And I play tennis three times a week.
STEPH Tennis? That sounds like a lot of fun.
MICK Oh, do you want to play sometime?
STEPH Uh . . . how well do you play?
MICK Pretty well, I guess.
STEPH Well, all right. But I'm not very good.
MICK No problem. I'll give you a few tips.

B Listen to Mick and Steph after their tennis match. Who's the winner?

11 GRAMMAR FOCUS

Questions with *how*; short answers

How often do you work out?
Every day.
Twice a week.
Not very often.

How long do you spend at the gym?
Thirty minutes a day.
Two hours a week.
About an hour on weekends.

How well do you play tennis?
Pretty well.
About average.
Not very well.

How good are you at sports?
Pretty good.
OK.
Not so good.

GRAMMAR PLUS *see page 137*

A Complete these questions. Then practice with a partner.

1. **A:** _____________ at sports?
   B: I guess I'm pretty good. I play a lot of different sports.
2. **A:** _____________ spend online?
   B: About an hour after dinner. I like to chat with my friends.
3. **A:** _____________ go to the beach?
   B: Once or twice a month. It's a good way to relax.
4. **A:** _____________ swim?
   B: Not very well. I need to take swimming lessons.

B GROUP WORK Take turns asking the questions in part A. Give your own information when answering. Then ask more questions with *how often*, *how long*, *how well*, and *how good*.

12 LISTENING You're in great shape!

Listen to Rachel, Nicholas, Zack, and Jennifer discuss sports and exercise. Who is a couch potato? a fitness freak? a sports nut? a gym rat?

a couch potato

1. _____________

a fitness freak

2. _____________

a sports nut

3. _____________

a gym rat

4. _____________

13 INTERCHANGE 6 What's your talent?

Find out how well your classmates do different activities. Go to Interchange 6 on page 120.

14 READING

A How healthy and fit do you think you are? Skim the questions. Then guess your health and fitness score from 0 (very unhealthy) to 50 (very healthy).

FIT AND HEALTHY?

Take the quiz!

1. How many servings of fruits or vegetables do you eat each day?

Five or more.	5
Between one and four.	3
I don't eat fruits or vegetables.	0

2. How much sugar do you use in food and drinks?

I hardly ever use sugar in my food and drink.	5
A little, but I'm careful.	3
A lot. I love sugar!	0

3. How often do you eat junk food?

Never.	5
Maybe once a week.	3
As often as possible.	0

4. How many glasses of water do you drink each day?

Eight or more.	5
Between one and three.	3
I almost always drink soda.	0

5. Do you eat oily fish (for example, sardines, salmon)?

Yes, I love fish!	5
Yes, about twice a month.	3
No, I really don't like fish.	0

6. How often do you exercise?

I usually exercise every day.	5
Two or three times a week.	3
What's exercise?	0

7. Do you walk or bike to work or school?

Yes, whenever I can.	5
I do when I have time.	3
No, never.	0

8. Is fitness important to you?

Yes, it's extremely important.	5
I think it's pretty important.	3
No, it's not important at all.	0

9. What do you do on weekends?

I play as many kinds of sports as I can!	5
I sometimes go for walks or bike rides.	3
I watch TV all day long.	0

10. When you're at work or school, how active are you?

Very active. I walk around a lot.	5
A little active. I go for a walk at lunchtime.	3
I sit at my desk and order lunch.	0

RATE YOURSELF!

42 to 50: Good job! You're doing all the right things for a healthy life.

28 to 41: You're on the right track. With a little more work, you'll be great.

15 to 27: Keep trying! You can be very fit and healthy, so don't give up!

14 or below: It's time to improve your health and fitness. You can do it!

B Take the quiz and add up your score. Is your score similar to your original guess? Do you agree with your score? Why or why not?

C **GROUP WORK** Compare your scores. Who is healthy and fit? What can your classmates do to improve their health and fitness?

Units 5–6 Progress check

SELF-ASSESSMENT

How well can you do these things? Check (✓) the boxes.

I can . . .	Very well	OK	A little
Ask about and describe present activities (Ex. 1, 2, 3)	☐	☐	☐
Describe family life (Ex. 3)	☐	☐	☐
Ask for and give personal information (Ex. 3)	☐	☐	☐
Give information about quantities (Ex. 3)	☐	☐	☐
Ask and answer questions about free time (Ex. 4)	☐	☐	☐
Ask and answer questions about routines and abilities (Ex. 4)	☐	☐	☐

1 LISTENING What are they doing?

A Listen to people do different things. What are they doing? Complete the chart.

B **PAIR WORK** Compare your answers.

A: In number one, someone is watching TV.
B: I don't think so. I think someone is . . .

What are they doing?
1. ______________________
2. ______________________
3. ______________________
4. ______________________

2 SPEAKING Memory game

GROUP WORK Choose a person in the room, but don't say who! Other students ask yes/no questions to guess the person.

A: I'm thinking of someone in the classroom.
B: Is it a man?
A: Yes, it is.
C: Is he sitting in the front of the room?
A: No, he isn't.
D: Is he sitting in the back?
A: Yes, he is.
E: Is he wearing a black T-shirt?
A: No, he isn't.
B: Is it . . . ?

The student with the correct guess has the next turn.

3 SPEAKING Family life survey

A GROUP WORK Add two more yes/no questions about family life to the chart. Then ask and answer the questions in groups. Write down the number of "yes" and "no" answers. (Remember to include yourself.)

	Number of "yes" answers	Number of "no" answers
1. Are you living with your family?		
2. Do your parents both work?		
3. Do you eat dinner with your family?		
4. Are you exercising these days?		
5. Are you studying something these days?		
6. Do you have brothers or sisters?		
7. ______________________		
8. ______________________		

B GROUP WORK Write up the results of the survey. Then tell the class.

1. In our group, most people are living with their families.
2. Nearly all of our mothers and fathers work.

Quantifiers

All	100%
Nearly all	
Most	
Many	
A lot of	
Some	
Not many	
Few	
No one	0%

4 DISCUSSION Routines and abilities

GROUP WORK Choose three questions. Then ask your questions in groups. When someone answers "yes," think of more questions to ask.

Do you ever . . . ?

- ☐ cook for friends
- ☐ do yoga
- ☐ go jogging
- ☐ listen to English songs
- ☐ play video games
- ☐ play volleyball
- ☐ sing in the shower
- ☐ tell jokes
- ☐ write emails in English

A: Do you ever cook for friends?
B: Yes, I often do.
C: What do you cook?
B: I usually cook fish or pasta.
A: When do you cook?
B: On weekends.
C: How often do you cook?
B: Once a month.
A: How well do you cook?
B: About average. But they always ask for more!

WHAT'S NEXT?

Look at your Self-assessment again. Do you need to review anything?

7 We went dancing!

- Describe past daily and free-time activities
- Describe past vacations

1 SNAPSHOT

Free-time Activities

☐ check social media

☐ go dancing

☐ listen to music

☐ play video games

☐ read

☐ relax

☐ spend time with friends and family

☐ watch TV

Check (✓) the activities you do in your free time. List three other activities you do in your free time.
What are your favorite free-time activities? Are there activities you don't like? Which ones?

2 CONVERSATION What did you do last weekend?

A Listen and practice.

NEIL So, what did you do last weekend, Cara?

CARA Oh, I had a great time. My friends and I had pizza on Saturday and then we all went dancing.

NEIL How fun! Did you go to The Treadmill?

CARA No, we didn't. We went to that new place downtown. How about you? Did you go anywhere?

NEIL No, I didn't go anywhere all weekend. I just stayed home and studied for today's Spanish test.

CARA Our test is today? I forgot about that!

NEIL Don't worry. You always get an A.

B Listen to the rest of the conversation. What does Cara do on Sunday afternoons?

3 GRAMMAR FOCUS

Simple past

Did you **work** on Saturday?
Yes, I **did**. I **worked** all day.
No, I **didn't**. I **didn't work** at all.

Did you **go** anywhere last weekend?
Yes, I **did**. I **went** to the movies.
No, I **didn't**. I **didn't go** anywhere.

What **did** Neil **do** on Saturday?
He **stayed** home and **studied** for a test.

How **did** Cara **spend** her weekend?
She **went** to a club and **danced** with some friends.

GRAMMAR PLUS *see page 138*

A Complete these conversations. Then practice with a partner.

1. **A:** ______________ you ______________ (stay) home on Sunday?
   B: No, I ______________ (call) my friend Anna. We ______________ (drive) to a nice little restaurant for lunch.
2. **A:** How ______________ you ______________ (spend) your last birthday?
   B: I ______________ (have) a party. Everyone ______________ (enjoy) it, but the neighbors next door ______________ (not, like) the noise.
3. **A:** What ______________ you ______________ (do) last night?
   B: I ______________ (see) a sci-fi movie at the Cineplex. I ______________ (love) it! Amazing special effects!
4. **A:** ______________ you ______________ (do) anything special over the weekend?
   B: Yes, I ______________. I ______________ (go) shopping. Unfortunately, I ______________ (spend) all my money. Now I'm broke!
5. **A:** ______________ you ______________ (go) out on Friday night?
   B: No, I ______________. I ______________ (invite) friends over, and I ______________ (cook) spaghetti for them.

regular verbs

work ⟶ work**ed**
invite ⟶ invit**ed**
study ⟶ stud**ied**
stop ⟶ stop**ped**

irregular verbs

buy ⟶ **bought**
do ⟶ **did**
drive ⟶ **drove**
have ⟶ **had**
go ⟶ **went**
sing ⟶ **sang**
see ⟶ **saw**
spend ⟶ **spent**

B **PAIR WORK** Take turns asking the questions in part A. Give your own information when answering.

A: Did you stay home on Sunday?
B: No, I didn't. I went dancing with some friends.

4 PRONUNCIATION Reduction of *did you*

A Listen and practice. Notice how **did you** is reduced in the following questions.

[dɪdʒə]
Did you have a good time?

[wədɪdʒə]
What did you do last night?

[haʊdɪdʒə]
How did you like the movie?

B **PAIR WORK** Practice the questions in Exercise 3, part A again. Pay attention to the pronunciation of **did you**.

5 WORD POWER Chores and activities

A **PAIR WORK** Find two other words or phrases from the list that usually go with each verb. Then add one more word or phrase to each verb.

a lot of fun	dancing	a good time	shopping	a bike ride
the bed	chores	the laundry	a trip	a video

do	*my homework*			
go	*online*			
have	*a party*			
make	*a phone call*			
take	*a day off*			

B **GROUP WORK** Choose the things you did last weekend. Then compare with your partners.

A: I went shopping with my friends. We had a good time. What about you?
B: I didn't have a very good time. I did chores.
C: I did chores, too. But I went dancing in the evening, and . . .

6 DISCUSSION Ask some questions!

GROUP WORK Take turns. One student makes a statement about the weekend. Other students ask questions. Each student answers at least three questions.

A: I went shopping on Saturday afternoon.
B: **Where** did you go?
A: To the Mayfair Center.
C: **Who** did you go with?
A: I went with my friends and my sister.
D: **What time** did you go?
A: We went around 3:00.

7 LISTENING Did you have a good holiday?

A Listen to Andrew tell Elizabeth what he did yesterday. Check (✓) the things Andrew did.

Activities	Reasons
☐ went to the gym	
☐ played soccer	
☐ saw a movie	
☐ watched TV	
☐ went to a baseball game	
☐ spent time with family	

B Listen again. Look at the activities Andrew didn't do. Why didn't he do them? Write the reason.

8 INTERCHANGE 7 Memories

Play a board game. Go to Interchange 7 on page 121.

9 CONVERSATION Lucky you!

A Listen and practice.

Leah: Hi, Cody. How was your vacation?

Cody: It was excellent! I went to California with my cousin. We had a great time.

Leah: Lucky you! How long were you there?

Cody: About a week.

Leah: Cool! Was the weather OK?

Cody: Not really. It was pretty cloudy. But we went surfing every day. The waves were amazing.

Leah: So, what was the best thing about the trip?

Cody: Well, something incredible happened. . . .

B Listen to the rest of the conversation. What happened?

10 GRAMMAR FOCUS

Past of *be*

		Contractions
Were you in California?	Yes, I **was**.	was**n't** = was **not**
Was the weather OK?	No, it **wasn't**.	were**n't** = were **not**
Were you and your cousin on vacation?	Yes, we **were**.	
Were your parents there?	No, they **weren't**.	
How long **were** you away?	I **was** away for a week.	
How **was** your vacation?	It **was** excellent!	

GRAMMAR PLUS *see page 138*

Complete these conversations. Then practice with a partner.

1. **A:** ______________ you in New York last weekend?
   B: No, I ______________ . I ______________ in Chicago.
   A: How ______________ it?
   B: It ______________ great! But it ______________ cold and windy as usual.
2. **A:** How long ______________ your parents in Chile?
   B: They ______________ there for two weeks.
   A: ______________ they in Santiago the whole time?
   B: No, they ______________ . They also went to Valparaiso.
3. **A:** ______________ you away last week?
   B: Yes, I ______________ in Madrid.
   A: Really? How long ______________ you there?
   B: For almost a week. I ______________ there on business.

11 DISCUSSION Past and future vacations

A **GROUP WORK** Ask your classmates about their last vacations. Ask these questions or use your own ideas.

Where did you spend your last vacation?
How long was your vacation?
Who were you with?
What did you do?
How was the weather?
What would you like to do on your next vacation?

B **CLASS ACTIVITY** Who had an interesting vacation? Tell the class who and why.

12 WRITING A blog post

A Read the blog post.

TRAVEL BLOG   Home   About   Posts   Subscribe

Greetings from sunny Puerto Vallarta, Mexico! I'm having a great time. Yesterday, I took a tour of the old town. The buildings and monuments were amazing! This morning, I went swimming and snorkeling. Then I went shopping at one of the town's open markets. I bought a very beautiful handmade ceramic vase and tried the famous fish on a stick. Delicious!

I'm having a really great vacation!

Casey

B **PAIR WORK** Write a blog post to your partner about your last vacation. Then exchange posts. Do you have any questions about your partner's vacation?

13 LISTENING I was on vacation.

A Listen to Daniel and Amanda talk about their vacations. Did they have a good time? Check (✓) Yes or No.

	Yes	No
Daniel	☐	☐
Amanda	☐	☐

B Listen again. Complete the chart with information about their vacations.

Daniel's vacation		Amanda's vacation	
Place		Place	
Who with		Who with	
Activities		Activities	

14 READING

A Look at the pictures. What do you think each person did on his or her vacation?

Profile Photos Share Friends

Awesome Vacations

1

Marco Tianzi Mountains

I came to this awesome place three days ago. These are the Tianzi Mountains, in Hunan Province, China. The mountains cover 67 square kilometers (or over 16,000 acres), and they are named for a famous farmer who lived in the area. I took a cable car up to the mountains. The ride was about six minutes long. The views are breathtaking! The mountains look almost like they are man-made. Sadly, my trip is almost over and I have to go home. But I want to come back soon!

2

Letitia Desert Breath

Guys, look at this! This is in the desert near Hurghada, Egypt. I was just there with my friend Carla. Desert Breath is a piece of land art made by three people in the nineties – an artist, an architect, and an engineer. It's made of sand, and it covers a large area of the Sahara Desert – 100,000 square meters (or about 25 acres). Every year, some of the art disappears. The wind moves the sand away. For now, it's so large that satellites in space take photos of it. How cool is that?

3

Kelly Giant Salt Lake

I flew from La Paz to Uyuni to see this spectacular place. I took so many pictures. It's called Salar de Uyuni, and it's in beautiful Bolivia. It was part of a giant salt lake in prehistoric times. I went there in a group with a guide. You have to walk a lot, so you need to be in pretty good shape. We walked for a whole day! Sometimes you feel like you're walking on clouds. When I saw the lake, it looked like a giant mirror. I'll never forget it!

B Read the online posts. Then write the number of the post where each sentence could go.

_____ It was pretty tiring, but I enjoyed every minute of it.
_____ The ride was scary because we were so high up.
_____ I hope to meet the people who made it.

C **PAIR WORK** Answer these questions.

1. Which person used an unusual form of transportation?
2. Who saw a piece of art?
3. Who had a very active vacation?
4. Which place do you think is the most interesting? Why?

8 How's the neighborhood?

- Ask about and describe places
- Describe a neighborhood

1 WORD POWER Places and activities

A Match the places and the definitions. Then ask and answer the questions with a partner.

What's a . . . ?	*It's a place where you . . .*
1. clothing store ______	**a.** get food and small items for the home
2. grocery store ______	**b.** can connect to the Internet
3. hair salon ______	**c.** get a haircut
4. laundromat ______	**d.** buy newspapers and magazines
5. newsstand ______	**e.** see a game or a concert
6. stadium ______	**f.** find new fashions
7. Wi-Fi hot spot ______	**g.** wash and dry your clothes

B **PAIR WORK** Write definitions for these places.

coffee shop **drugstore** **gas station** **library** **post office**

It's a place where you drink coffee and tea and eat small meals. (coffee shop)

C **GROUP WORK** Read your definitions. Can your classmates guess the places?

2 CONVERSATION I just moved in.

Listen and practice.

Greg Excuse me! Hi, I'm your new neighbor, Greg. I just moved in.

Mrs. Cook Oh. Yes?

Greg I'm looking for a grocery store. Are there any around here?

Mrs. Cook Yes, there are some on Pine Street.

Greg Oh, good. And is there a laundromat near here?

Mrs. Cook Well, I think there's one across from the shopping center.

Greg Thank you.

Mrs. Cook By the way, there's a hair salon in the shopping center.

Greg A hair salon?

3 GRAMMAR FOCUS

There is, there are; one, any, some

Is there a laundromat near here?
Yes, **there is**. There's **one** across from the shopping center.
No, **there isn't**, but there's **one** next to the library.

Are there any grocery stores around here?
Yes, **there are**. There are **some** nice stores on Pine Street.
No, **there aren't**, but there are **some** on Third Avenue.
No, **there aren't any** around here.

Prepositions
in
on
next to
near/close to
across from/opposite
in front of
in back of/behind
between
on the corner of

GRAMMAR PLUS see page 139

A Look at the map below. Write questions about these places.

an ATM	coffee shops	a department store	an electronics store	Wi-Fi hot spots
gas stations	grocery stores	a gym	hotels	a post office

Is there a gym around here?
Are there any restaurants on Main Street?

B **PAIR WORK** Ask and answer the questions you wrote in part A.

A: Is there a gym around here?
B: Yes, there is. There's one on Main Street next to the post office.

4 PRONUNCIATION Reduction of *there is/there are*

A Listen and practice. Notice how *there is* and *there are* are reduced in conversation, except for short answers.

Is there a bank near here?
Yes, **there is**. **There's** one on First Avenue.

Are there any coffee shops around here?
Yes, **there are**. **There are** some on Pine Street.

B Practice the questions and answers in Exercise 3, part B again.

5 SPEAKING A nice neighborhood

A **PAIR WORK** Choose a neighborhood in your city or town. Fill in the chart with information about the neighborhood. Write three examples for each category. Go to Exercises 1 and 3 for ideas and use your own ideas, too.

There is a/an . . . (where?)	There are some . . . (where?)
There isn't a/an . . . (where?)	**There aren't any . . . (where?)**

B **GROUP WORK** Take turns asking and answering questions with another pair about the neighborhoods. If you don't know about a place your new partners ask about, answer, "Sorry, I don't know." Who gets more "Yes" answers?

A: Is there a gym in your neighborhood?
B: Yes, there's one across from the park.
C: Are there any coffee shops?
D: No, there aren't any in our neighborhood.
B: Is there a bookstore in your neighborhood?
A: Sorry, I don't know.

6 LISTENING We need some directions.

A Listen to hotel guests ask about places to visit. Complete the chart.

Place	Location	Interesting? Yes	Interesting? No
Flavors of Hollywood		☐	☐
Museum of Modern Art		☐	☐
City Zoo		☐	☐

B **PAIR WORK** Which place sounds the most interesting to you? Why?

7 SNAPSHOT

What types of businesses are or aren't found in these neighborhoods?
Which areas do you visit often? Which areas do you hardly ever visit? Why?

8 CONVERSATION It's very convenient.

Listen and practice.

BARRY How do you like your new apartment, Alana?

ALANA I love it. It's downtown, so it's very convenient.

BARRY Downtown? Is there much traffic?

ALANA Yeah, there's a lot. But I don't drive, so it's OK.

BARRY Oh, that's right. Is there much crime in the area?

ALANA No, it's pretty safe. The difference is the noise.

BARRY Really? Is there a lot of noise?

ALANA There's a lot on the weekend from the Italian restaurant downstairs.

BARRY Oh, that's too bad. But is the food at the restaurant good?

ALANA It's incredible! Hey, would you like to have dinner there on Saturday?

BARRY Yes! I love Italian food.

9 GRAMMAR FOCUS

Quantifiers; *how many* and *how much*

Count nouns	Noncount nouns
Are there **many restaurants**?	Is there **much crime**?
Yes, there are **a lot**.	Yes, there's **a lot**.
There are **a few**.	There's **a little**.
No, there are**n't many**.	No, there is**n't much**.
No, there are**n't any**.	No, there is**n't any**.
No, there are **none**.	No, there's **none**.
How many restaurants are there?	**How much** crime is there?
There are 10 or 12.	There's a lot of crime.

GRAMMAR PLUS *see page 139*

A Write answers to these questions about your neighborhood. Then practice with a partner.

1. Is there much parking?
2. Are there many apartment buildings?
3. How much traffic is there?
4. How many drugstores are there?
5. Is there much noise?
6. Are there many shopping malls?
7. Is there much pollution?
8. How many fast-food restaurants are there?

B **GROUP WORK** Write questions like those in part A about these topics. Then ask and answer the questions.

cafés crime parks trash public transportation schools traffic lights

10 INTERCHANGE 8 Where are we?

Play a guessing game. Go to Interchange 8 on page 122.

11 WRITING My neighborhood

A Read this paragraph Kate wrote about her neighborhood.

B Now write a paragraph about your neighborhood. Describe what type of neighborhood it is and what places are or aren't in your area.

C **PAIR WORK** Read your partner's paragraph. Ask follow-up questions to get more information.

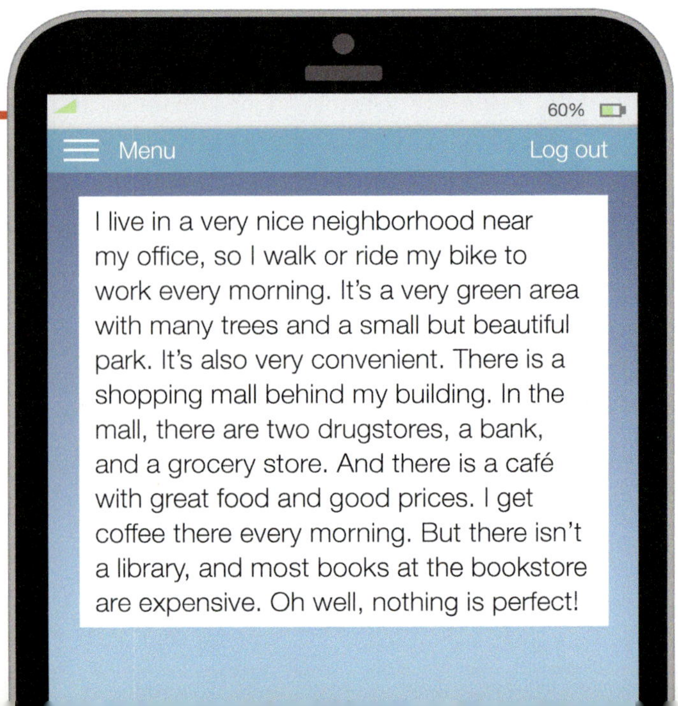

I live in a very nice neighborhood near my office, so I walk or ride my bike to work every morning. It's a very green area with many trees and a small but beautiful park. It's also very convenient. There is a shopping mall behind my building. In the mall, there are two drugstores, a bank, and a grocery store. And there is a café with great food and good prices. I get coffee there every morning. But there isn't a library, and most books at the bookstore are expensive. Oh well, nothing is perfect!

12 READING

A Scan the article. Check (✓) the neighborhood that is famous for nightlife.

☐ Roma Norte ☐ Shimokitazawa ☐ Pigneto

Locations Reservations Shop Sign in Register

HIP NEIGHBORHOODS OF THE WORLD

A Shimokitazawa, Tokyo

This is the place to be for fans of indie music! Head over to this creative neighborhood and discover record stores, concert halls, and theaters in the narrow streets. Shimokitazawa (or Shimokita, for short) is a relaxed place full of young people who visit the cafés and live music venues. Every year, there is a theater festival here. It's a very popular place for students.

B Pigneto, Rome

La Sapienza, a famous college in Rome, is near this neighborhood. It's an extremely cool place to hang out. Pigneto has a huge choice of restaurants, cafés, and ice cream stores. Pigneto is famous for its nightlife. As you walk around, you hear electronic music coming from different clubs. People also come here for the Nuovo Cinema Aquila, the best place to see indie movies from around the world.

C Roma Norte, Mexico City

This place is popular with artists, students, tourists, and musicians. Feeling hungry? Go to a huge food market, Mercado Roma, to taste delicious ceviche, squid torta, and other Mexican specialties. Next, check out the trendy restaurants for dinner, or shop for beautiful fashion items in the boutiques. There are hip T-shirts and sneakers for sale everywhere. There's locally made jewelry you can buy, too!

B Read the article. Then write the letter of the paragraph where these things are mentioned.

1. ______ local jewelry
2. ______ festivals
3. ______ indie movies
4. ______ record stores
5. ______ food specialties
6. ______ a college
7. ______ theaters
8. ______ ice cream

C **PAIR WORK** What's your favorite neighborhood in your city or country? What is interesting about it? What do you like to do there?

Units 7–8 Progress check

SELF-ASSESSMENT

How well can you do these things? Check (✓) the boxes.

I can . . .	Very well	OK	A little
Understand descriptions of past events (Ex. 1)	☐	☐	☐
Describe events in the past (Ex. 1)	☐	☐	☐
Ask and answer questions about past activities (Ex. 2)	☐	☐	☐
Give and understand simple directions (Ex. 3)	☐	☐	☐
Talk about my neighborhood (Ex. 4)	☐	☐	☐

1 LISTENING Jimmy's weekend

A A thief robbed a house on Saturday. A detective is questioning Jimmy. The pictures show what Jimmy really did on Saturday. Listen to their conversation. Are Jimmy's answers true (**T**) or false (**F**)?

1:00 P.M. T F　3:00 P.M. T F　5:00 P.M. T F　6:00 P.M. T F　8:00 P.M. T F　10:30 P.M. T F

B **PAIR WORK** What did Jimmy really do? Use the pictures to retell the story.

2 DISCUSSION How good is your memory?

A Do you remember what you did yesterday? Check (✓) the things you did. Then add two other things you did.

- ☐ got up early
- ☐ exercised
- ☐ texted a friend
- ☐ went to class
- ☐ ate at a restaurant
- ☐ went shopping
- ☐ did the laundry
- ☐ did the dishes
- ☐ went online
- ☐ went to bed late
- ☐ ____________
- ☐ ____________

B **GROUP WORK** Ask questions about each thing in part A.

A: Did you get up early yesterday?
B: No, I didn't. I got up at 10:00. I was very tired.

3 SPEAKING What's your neighborhood like?

A Create a neighborhood. Add five places to "My map." Choose from this list. Add plural words two or more times.

a bank **a bookstore** **cafés** **drugstores** **gas stations** **a gym** **a theater**

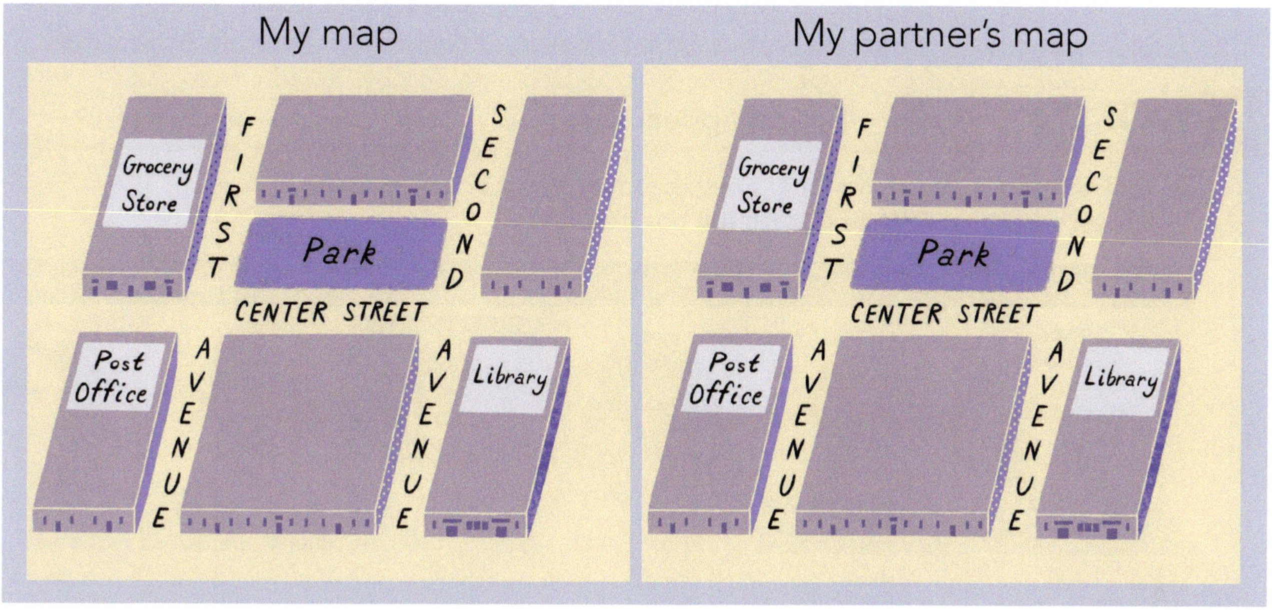

B **PAIR WORK** Ask questions about your partner's map. (But don't look!) Draw the places on "My partner's map." Then compare your maps.

A: Are there any gas stations in the neighborhood?
B: Yes, there are two. There's one on the corner of Center Street and First Avenue and one on Center Street across from the park.

4 ROLE PLAY Tell me about your neighborhood.

Student A: Imagine you are a visitor in Student B's neighborhood. Ask questions about it.

Student B: Imagine a visitor wants to find out about your neighborhood. Answer the visitor's questions.

A: Is there much crime?
B: There isn't much. It's a very safe neighborhood.
A: Is there much noise?
B: Well, yes, it's a shopping district, so . . .

Change roles and try the role play again.

topics to ask about

- buildings
- crime
- noise
- parking
- parks
- places to shop
- pollution
- public transportation
- schools
- traffic

WHAT'S NEXT?

Look at your Self-assessment again. Do you need to review anything?

9 What does she look like?

- Describe people's physical appearance
- Identify people by describing how they look and what they're doing

1 WORD POWER Physical appearance

A Look at these expressions. What are three more words or expressions to describe people? Write them in the box below.

HAIR

long brown hair | short blond hair | straight black hair | curly red hair | bald | a mustache and a beard

AGE

young | middle-aged | elderly

LOOKS

handsome | good-looking | pretty

HEIGHT

short | fairly short | medium height | pretty tall | very tall

Other words or expressions

B **PAIR WORK** Choose at least four expressions to describe yourself and your partner. Then compare. Do you agree?

A: You have long blond hair. You're pretty tall.
B: I don't think so. My hair isn't very long.

Me	My partner

2 CONVERSATION She's so pretty!

A Listen and practice.

Lauren: I hear you have a new girlfriend, Justin.
Justin: Yes. Her name's Tiffany. She's really smart, and she's so pretty!
Lauren: Really? What does she look like?
Justin: Well, she's very tall.
Lauren: How tall?
Justin: About 5 foot 10, I suppose.
Lauren: Yeah, that *is* pretty tall. What color is her hair?
Justin: She has beautiful brown hair.
Lauren: And how old is she?
Justin: I don't know. I think it's a little rude to ask.

B Listen to the rest of the conversation. What else do you learn about Tiffany?

3 GRAMMAR FOCUS

Describing people

General appearance	Height	Hair	Age
What does she look like?	How tall is she?	How long is her hair?	How old is she?
She's tall, with brown hair.	She's 1 meter 78.	It's pretty short.	She's about 32.
She's pretty.	She's 5 foot 10.		She's in her thirties.
Does he wear glasses?	How tall is he?	What color is his hair?	How old is he?
No, he wears contacts.	He's medium height.	It's dark/light brown.	He's in his twenties.

Saying heights

	U.S.	Metric
	five (foot) ten.	one meter seventy-eight tall.
Tiffany is	five foot ten inches (tall).	1 meter 78.
	5'10".	178 cm.

GRAMMAR PLUS *see page 140*

A Write questions to match these statements. Then compare with a partner.

1. ______________________________? My father is 52.
2. ______________________________? I'm 167 cm (5 foot 6).
3. ______________________________? My cousin has red hair.
4. ______________________________? No, he wears contact lenses.
5. ______________________________? He's tall and very good-looking.
6. ______________________________? My sister's hair is medium length.
7. ______________________________? I have dark brown eyes.

B **PAIR WORK** Choose a person in your class. Don't tell your partner who it is. Your partner will ask questions to guess the person's name.

A: Is it a man or a woman?
B: It's a man.

A: What color is his hair?
B: . . .

4 LISTENING Which one is Justin?

A Listen to descriptions of six people. Number them from 1 to 6.

B Listen again. How old is each person?

5 INTERCHANGE 9 Find the differences

Compare two pictures of a party. Student A go to Interchange 9A on page 123. Student B go to Interchange 9B on page 124.

6 WRITING Describing physical appearance

A You are helping to organize a special event at your school with sports, arts, and a surprise celebrity guest. Write an email to a friend inviting him or her to the event, and describe the celebrity. Don't give the celebrity's name.

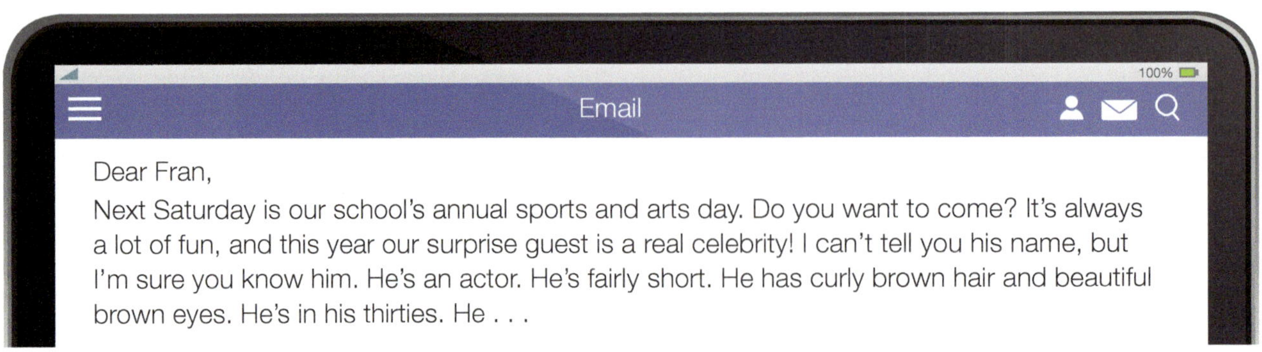

B **GROUP WORK** Read your email to the group. Can they guess the celebrity you are describing?

7 SNAPSHOT

New York *Street Fashion*

Boho (Bohemian)

The boho girl wears comfortable clothes – long skirts and flowy dresses in colorful floral prints.

Classic Prep

The preppy guy wears shirts and sweaters in pastel colors, khaki pants, and leather belts.

Hipster

The hipster wears hip hats, jewelry, and large glasses. Black is a popular color. The men often have unique hairstyles and long beards.

Streetwear

The streetwear fan wears casual and trendy clothes: jeans, basketball jerseys, baseball caps, T-shirts with logos, and cool sneakers.

Do you see your style(s)? Which one(s)?
Which style(s) do you like? Which do you dislike? Why?
Do you see any of these styles on the streets in your town or city? Which one(s)?

8 CONVERSATION Which one is she?

A Listen and practice.

Brooke: Hi, Diego! Good to see you! Is Cora here, too?
Diego: Oh, she couldn't make it. She went to a concert with Alanna.
Brooke: Oh! Let's go talk to my friend Paula. She doesn't know anyone here.
Diego: Paula? Which one is she? Is she the woman wearing a long skirt over there?
Brooke: No, she's the tall one in jeans and a scarf. She's standing near the window.
Diego: OK. I'd like to meet her.

B Listen to the rest of the conversation. Label Liam, Hina, Sierra, and Matt in the picture.

9 GRAMMAR FOCUS

Modifiers with present participles and prepositions

		Participles
Who's Diego?	He's **the man**	**wearing** a blue shirt.
Which one is Diego?	He's **the one**	**talking** to Brooke.
		Prepositions
Who's Brooke?	She's **the woman**	**with** long black hair.
Which one is Paula?	She's **the tall one**	**in** jeans.
Who are the Harrisons?	They're **the people**	**next to** the window.
Which ones are the Harrisons?	They're **the ones**	**on** the couch.

GRAMMAR PLUS *see page 140*

A Rewrite these statements using modifiers with participles or prepositions.

1. Kyle is the tall guy. He's wearing a yellow shirt and brown pants.
   Kyle is the tall guy wearing a yellow shirt and brown pants.
2. Mark and Eve are the middle-aged couple. They're talking to Michael.
   ____
3. Alexis is the young girl. She's in a white T-shirt and blue jeans.
   ____
4. Britney is the woman in the green dress. She's sitting to the left of Javier.
   ____
5. J.P. is the serious-looking boy. He's playing a video game.
   ____

B **PAIR WORK** Complete these questions using your classmates' names and information. Then take turns asking and answering the questions.

1. Who's the guy (man) sitting next to ______________________________?
2. Who's the girl (woman) wearing ______________________________?
3. Who is ______________________________?
4. Which one is ______________________________?
5. Who are the people ______________________________?
6. Who are the ones ______________________________?

10 PRONUNCIATION Contrastive stress in responses

A Listen and practice. Notice how the stress changes to emphasize a contrast.

A: Is Rob the one wearing the red shirt?
B: No, he's the one wearing the black shirt.

A: Is Rachel the woman on the couch?
B: No, Jen is the woman on the couch.

B Mark the stress changes in these conversations. Listen and check. Then practice the conversations.

A: Is Sophie the one sitting next to Judy?
B: No, she's the one standing next to Judy.

A: Is David the one on the couch?
B: No, he's the one behind the couch.

11 READING

A Match the descriptions with the pictures. Write the letter.

This picture is out of this world! ______
My life in fashion. ______
An old idea meets the twenty-first century. ______
The real me or the "perfect" me? ______

THE AGE OF SELFIES

A

THE BIRTH OF THE SELFIE

Most of us take selfies now and then. Presidents, rock stars, actors, and sports stars all take them. It's very easy to take selfies on a smartphone. But the selfie isn't really a new idea. Back in 1839, a man named Robert Cornelius took the very first selfie. Cornelius was a photographer from Philadelphia, in the U.S. He took the picture of himself by setting up his camera and then running to stand in front of it. On the back of the picture, Cornelius wrote: "The first light picture ever taken. 1839."

B

WORLD'S BEST SELFIE?

Astronaut Aki Hoshide is the third Japanese astronaut to walk in space. But that's not the only reason he's famous. Hoshide created an amazing image! The astronaut took this picture while he was at the International Space Station. The photo shows him, the sun, and deep space in the same shot. He named it "Orbiting Astronaut Self-Portrait."

C

THE PSYCHOLOGY OF SELFIES

Why do people want to take pictures of themselves? Psychologists say that it's a way of understanding who we are. It's also a way of controlling how other people see us. When we take selfies, we can choose the flattering ones – the ones that make us look really good – and share them with our friends on social media or over text. Some people take their selfies very seriously. There are even apps people can use to make their faces look "perfect."

D

THE DAILY SELFIE

Several years ago, Poppy Dinsey started a fashion blog. She had a simple but great idea. Every day for a year she posted a selfie of herself wearing a different outfit. So one day, she's wearing jeans. Another day, she's wearing skinny pants and a baggy sweater. The next day, she's wearing a hip dress. People loved Poppy's blog. Many people started their own fashion blogs because they liked her so much.

B Read the blog. Match each question with the correct answer.

1. What is Poppy Dinsey famous for? _____
2. Where did Aki Hoshide take a selfie? _____
3. Who says selfies are a way of understanding ourselves? _____
4. Who took the first selfie? _____
5. Where do many people post selfies? _____
6. What is Hoshide's job? _____

a. at the International Space Station
b. astronaut
c. on social media
d. psychologists
e. a fashion blog
f. a man from Philadelphia

C **PAIR WORK** What do you think of selfies? When and where do you take selfies? What's the main reason you take selfies?

10 Have you ever been there?

- Describe recent activities
- Describe experiences from the recent and distant past

1 SNAPSHOT

Which activities have you done?
Check (✓) the activities you would like to try.
Where can you do these or similar activities in your country?

2 CONVERSATION My feet are killing me!

A Listen and practice.

Erin: It's great to see you again, Carlos! Have you been in Orlando long?
Carlos: You too, Erin! I've been here for about a week.
Erin: I can't wait to show you the city. Have you been to the theme parks yet?
Carlos: Yeah, I've already been to three. The lines were so long!
Erin: OK. Well, how about shopping? I know a great store. . .
Carlos: Well, I've already been to so many stores. I can't buy any more clothes.
Erin: I know what! I bet you haven't visited the Kennedy Space Center. It's an hour away.
Carlos: Actually, I've already been to the Space Center and met an astronaut!
Erin: Wow! You've done a lot! Well, is there anything you want to do?
Carlos: You know, I really just want to take it easy today. My feet are killing me!

B Listen to the rest of the conversation. What do they plan to do tomorrow?

3 GRAMMAR FOCUS

Present perfect; *already, yet*

The present perfect is formed with the verb *have* + the past participle.

Have you **been** to a jazz club?
Yes, I**'ve been** to several. No, I **haven't been** to one.
Has Carlos **visited** the theme parks?
Yes, he**'s visited** three or four. No, he **hasn't visited** any parks.
Have they **eaten** dinner yet?
Yes, they**'ve** already **eaten**. No, they **haven't eaten** yet.

Contractions

I**'ve**	=	I have
you**'ve**	=	you have
he**'s**	=	he has
she**'s**	=	she has
it**'s**	=	it has
we**'ve**	=	we have
they**'ve**	=	they have
has**n't**	=	has not
have**n't**	=	have not

GRAMMAR PLUS *see page 141*

A How many times have you done these things in the past week? Write your answers. Then compare with a partner.

1. cook dinner
2. wash the dishes
3. listen to music
4. do the laundry
5. go to a restaurant
6. clean the house

I've cooked dinner twice this week.
OR
I haven't cooked dinner this week.

regular past participles

visit	⟶	visited
like	⟶	liked
stop	⟶	stopped
try	⟶	tried

irregular past participles

be	⟶	been
do	⟶	done
eat	⟶	eaten
go	⟶	gone
have	⟶	had
hear	⟶	heard
make	⟶	made
ride	⟶	ridden
see	⟶	seen

B Complete these conversations using the present perfect. Then practice with a partner.

1. **A:** ___*Have*___ you ___*done*___ much exercise this week? (do)
   B: Yes, I ___________ already ___________ to Pilates class four times. (be)
2. **A:** ___________ you ___________ any sports this month? (play)
   B: No, I ___________ the time. (not have)
3. **A:** How many movies ___________ you ___________ to this month? (be)
   B: Actually, I ___________ any yet. (not see)
4. **A:** ___________ you ___________ to any interesting parties recently? (be)
   B: No, I ___________ to any parties for quite a while. (not go)
5. **A:** ___________ you ___________ any food this week? (cook)
   B: Yes, I ___________ already ___________ dinner twice. (make)
6. **A:** How many times ___________ you ___________ out to eat this week? (go)
   B: I ___________ at fast-food restaurants a couple of times. (eat)

C **PAIR WORK** Take turns asking the questions in part B. Give your own information when answering.

4 CONVERSATION Have you ever had a Cuban sandwich?

A Listen and practice.

Erin: I'm sorry I'm late. Have you been here long?

Carlos: No, only for a few minutes. So, have you chosen a restaurant yet?

Erin: I can't decide. We can go to a big restaurant or a have a sandwich at a café. Have you ever had a Cuban sandwich?

Carlos: No, I haven't. Are they good?

Erin: They're delicious. I've had them many times.

Carlos: You really like Cuban food! Have you ever been to Cuba?

Erin: No, but I went to college in Miami. I ate empanadas and rice and beans all the time!

B Listen to the rest of the conversation. Where do they decide to go after lunch?

5 GRAMMAR FOCUS

Present perfect vs. simple past

	Use the present perfect for an indefinite time in the past.	Use the simple past for a specific event in the past.
Have you ever **eaten** Cuban food?	Yes, I **have**. I**'ve had** it many times. No, I **haven't**. I **haven't tried** it yet.	I **ate** a lot of Cuban food when I **lived** in Miami. No, I never **tried** it when I **lived** in Miami.
Have you ever **seen** an alligator?	Yes, I **have**. I**'ve seen** a few alligators in my life. No, I **haven't**. I**'ve** never **seen** one.	I **saw** a big alligator at the new park last week. I **didn't go** to the alligator park last week, so I **didn't see** any.

GRAMMAR PLUS *see page 141*

A Complete these conversations. Use the present perfect and simple past of the verbs given and short answers.

1. **A:** __________ you ever __________ in public? (sing)
   B: Yes, I __________. I __________ at a friend's birthday party.
2. **A:** __________ you ever __________ something valuable? (lose)
   B: No, I __________. But my brother __________ his cell phone on a trip once.
3. **A:** __________ you ever __________ a traffic ticket? (get)
   B: Yes, I __________. Once I __________ a ticket and had to pay $50.
4. **A:** __________ you ever __________ a live concert? (see)
   B: Yes, I __________. I __________ Adele at the stadium last year.
5. **A:** __________ you ever __________ late for an important event? (be)
   B: No, I __________. But my sister __________ two hours late for her wedding!

B **PAIR WORK** Take turns asking the questions in part A. Give your own information when answering.

For and *since*

How long **did** you **live** in Miami?	I **lived** there **for** four years. It was a great experience.
How long **have** you **lived** in Orlando?	I'**ve lived** here **for** three years. I'm very happy here. I'**ve worked** at the hotel **since** last year. I love it there.

GRAMMAR PLUS *see page 141*

C Complete these sentences with *for* or *since*. Then compare with a partner.

1. Maura was in Central America ____________ a month last year.
2. I've been a college student ____________ almost four years.
3. Hiroshi has been at work ____________ 6:00 A.M.
4. I haven't gone to a party ____________ a long time.
5. Sean lived in Bolivia ____________ two years as a kid.
6. My parents have been on vacation ____________ Monday.
7. Jennifer was engaged to Theo ____________ six months.
8. Alex and Brianna have been best friends ____________ high school.

expressions with *for*

two weeks
a few months
several years
a long time

expressions with *since*

6:45
last weekend
2009
elementary school

D **PAIR WORK** Ask and answer these questions.

How long have you had your current hairstyle?
How long have you studied at this school?
How long have you known your best friend?
How long have you been awake today?

6 PRONUNCIATION Linked sounds

A Listen and practice. Notice how final /t/ and /d/ sounds in verbs are linked to the vowels that follow them.

A: Have you cooked lunch yet?
B: Yes, I've already cooked it. (/t/)

A: Have you ever tried Key Lime Pie?
B: Yes, I tried it once in Miami. (/d/)

B **PAIR WORK** Ask and answer these questions. Use *it* in your responses. Pay attention to the linked sounds.

Have you ever cut your own hair?
Have you ever tasted blue cheese?
Have you ever tried Vietnamese food?
Have you ever lost your ID?
Have you looked at Unit 11 yet?

7 LISTENING Great to see you!

Listen to Nicole tell Tyler about some interesting things she's done recently. Complete the chart.

Places Nicole went	What she did there	Has Tyler been there before?
1.		☐ Yes ☐ No
2.		☐ Yes ☐ No

8 WORD POWER Life experiences

A Find two phrases to go with each verb. Write them in the chart.

a bike	your English books	a costume	a truck	your phone	a motorcycle
sushi	chocolate soda	iced coffee	octopus	a sports car	a uniform

eat			
drink			
drive			
lose			
ride			
wear			

B Add another phrase for each verb in part A.

9 SPEAKING Have you ever . . . ?

A **GROUP WORK** Ask your classmates questions about the activities in Exercise 8 or your own ideas.

A: Have you ever worn a costume?
B: Yes, I have.
C: Really? Where were you?

B **CLASS ACTIVITY** Tell the class one interesting thing you learned about a classmate.

10 WRITING An email to an old friend

A Write an email to someone you haven't seen for a long time. Include three things you've done since you last saw that person.

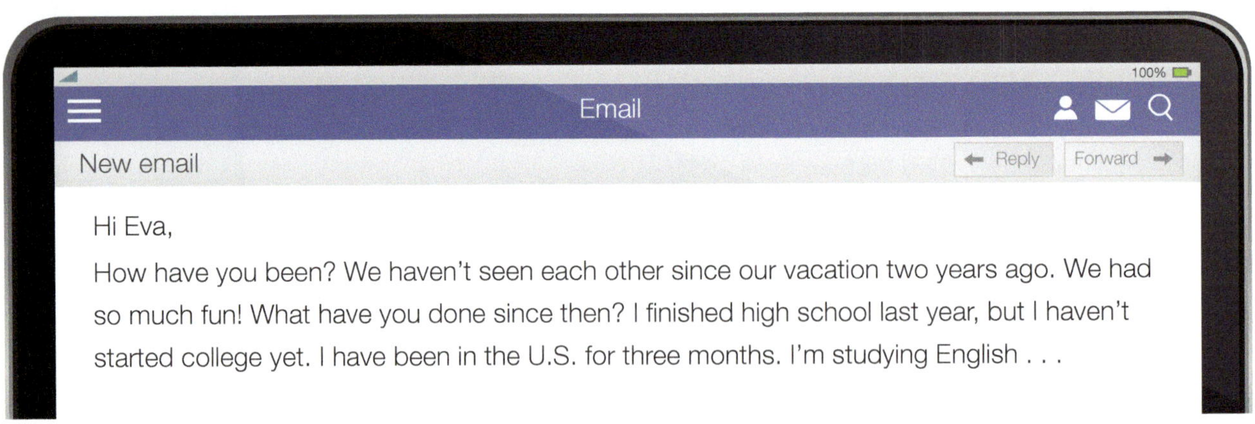

B **PAIR WORK** Exchange emails with a partner. Write a response about the three things your partner has done.

11 INTERCHANGE 10 Fun survey

How much fun do you have? Go to Interchange 10 on page 125.

12 READING

A Look at the photos. Skim the blog posts. What did Jennifer Aniston do in her sleep? How did Mervyn Kincaid cross the Irish Sea?

UNIQUE EXPERIENCES

How much is that pizza?!

Do you like pizza? Do you *really* like pizza? Do you like pizza enough to spend over $100 on one? Some people do! And here's the reason why. Truffles are similar to mushrooms, but they grow underground. They're extremely expensive. They can cost hundreds of dollars each. Pizza usually only costs a few dollars, but some people have paid as much as $178 to eat pizza with fresh white truffles on it. Celebrity TV chef Gordon Ramsay has won a place in the Guinness Book of Records for inventing this expensive dish.

Do you sleepwalk?

Did you know that some people walk in their sleep? Well, you probably do because it's a surprisingly common problem. In fact, almost a third of the U.S. population has sleepwalked at some point in their lives. The actress Jennifer Aniston is one of them. Jennifer has set off the burglar alarm in her own house by walking around while she was asleep.

Set sail in a bathtub!

Have you ever dreamed of going on a really big adventure? One man has crossed the Irish Sea . . . in a bathtub! Yes, you heard that right. Mervyn Kincaid has sailed from Ireland to Scotland in a bathtub with a small engine attached. Even better, Mervyn has raised a lot of money for charity. His friends and family have all made donations.

Oh no! I hit "send"!

Have you ever pushed "send" on a text message and then realized you've just sent a text to the wrong person? Hopefully not! But Burt Brown has. This 30-year-old software engineer has just sent 30 cute pictures of his baby to his boss instead of his mom! Luckily, his boss is a good guy and understood the mistake.

B Read the blog posts. Check (✓) True or False.

	True	False
1. Pizza is very expensive in the U.S.	☐	☐
2. Truffles grow underground.	☐	☐
3. Mervyn Kincaid didn't use a boat for his journey.	☐	☐
4. Mervyn Kincaid crossed the Irish Sea to pay for his bathtub.	☐	☐
5. Sleepwalking is extremely rare.	☐	☐
6. There was a lot of noise when Jennifer Aniston walked in her sleep.	☐	☐
7. Burt Brown sent photos to his boss.	☐	☐
8. Burt's boss was very angry about the baby pictures.	☐	☐

C **GROUP WORK** What unique experiences have you had in your life? Were they fun? Were they embarrassing? Tell your classmates.

Units 9–10 Progress check

SELF-ASSESSMENT

How well can you do these things? Check (✓) the boxes.

I can . . .	Very well	OK	A little
Ask about and describe people's appearance (Ex. 1)	☐	☐	☐
Identify people by describing what they're doing, what they're wearing, and where they are (Ex. 2)	☐	☐	☐
Find out whether or not things have been done (Ex. 3)	☐	☐	☐
Understand descriptions of experiences (Ex. 4)	☐	☐	☐
Ask and answer questions about experiences (Ex. 4)	☐	☐	☐
Find out how long people have done things (Ex. 5)	☐	☐	☐

1 ROLE PLAY Missing person

Student A: One of your classmates is lost. You are talking to a police officer. Answer the officer's questions and describe your classmate.

Student B: You are a police officer. Someone is describing a lost classmate. Ask questions to complete the form. Can you identify the classmate?

Change roles and try the role play again.

MISSING PERSON REPORT

NAME ______________________

HEIGHT: ________ WEIGHT: ________ AGE: ________

EYE COLOR:
- ☐ BLUE ☐ BROWN
- ☐ GREEN ☐ HAZEL

HAIR COLOR:
- ☐ BLOND ☐ BROWN
- ☐ RED ☐ BLACK
- ☐ GRAY ☐ BALD

CLOTHING: ______________________

GLASSES, ETC: ______________________

2 SPEAKING Which one is . . . ?

A Look at this picture. How many sentences can you write to identify the people?

Mia and Derek are the people in sunglasses.
They're the ones looking at the tablet.

B PAIR WORK Try to memorize the people in the picture. Then close your books. Take turns asking about the people.

A: Which one is Allen?
B: I think Allen is the guy eating . . .

3 SPEAKING "To do" lists

A Imagine you are preparing for these situations. Make a list of four things you need to do for each situation.

You are going to go to the beach this weekend.
Your first day of school is in a week.
You are going to move to a new apartment.

"To do" list: trip to the beach
1. buy a swimsuit

B **PAIR WORK** Exchange lists. Take turns asking about what has been done. When answering, decide what you have or haven't done.

A: Have you bought a swimsuit yet?
B: Yes, I've already gotten one.

4 LISTENING I won a contest!

A Alyssa has just met a friend in San Diego. Listen to her talk about things she has done. Check (✓) the correct things.

Alyssa has . . .	
☐ won a contest.	☐ gone windsurfing.
☐ flown in a plane.	☐ lost her wallet.
☐ stayed in an expensive hotel.	☐ gotten sunburned.
☐ met a famous person.	☐ posted on a blog.

B **GROUP WORK** Have you ever done the things in part A? Take turns asking about each thing.

5 SURVEY How long have you . . .?

A Add one more question to the chart. Write answers to these questions using *for* and *since*.

How long have you . . . ?	My answers	Classmate's name
owned this book		
studied English		
known your teacher		
lived in this town or city		
been a student		
______________		

B **CLASS ACTIVITY** Go around the class. Find someone who has the same answers. Write a classmate's name only once.

WHAT'S NEXT?

Look at your Self-assessment again. Do you need to review anything?

11 It's a really nice city.

- Describe hometowns, cities, and countries
- Make recommendations about places to visit

1 WORD POWER Adjectives to describe places

A PAIR WORK Match each word in column A with its opposite in column B. Then add two more pairs of adjectives to the list.

A	B
1. beautiful	**a.** boring
2. cheap	**b.** crowded
3. clean	**c.** dangerous
4. interesting	**d.** expensive
5. quiet	**e.** noisy
6. relaxing	**f.** polluted
7. safe	**g.** stressful
8. spacious	**h.** ugly
9. ______	**i.** ______
10. ______	**j.** ______

beautiful

ugly

B PAIR WORK Choose two places you know. Describe them to your partner using the words in part A.

2 CONVERSATION It looks so relaxing.

A Listen and practice.

Ron: That photo is really cool! Where is that?

Camila: That's a beach near my house in Punta Cana, in the Dominican Republic.

Ron: It looks so relaxing. I've heard the area is really beautiful.

Camila: Yeah, it is. The weather is great, and there are some fantastic beaches. The water is really clear, too.

Ron: Is it expensive there?

Camila: Well, it's not cheap. But prices for tourists can be pretty reasonable.

Ron: Hmm . . . and how far is it from Santo Domingo?

Camila: It's not *too* far from the capital. About 200 kilometers . . . a little over 120 miles.

Ron: It sounds very interesting. I should plan a trip there sometime.

Punta Cana, Dominican Republic

B Listen to the rest of the conversation. What does Camila say about entertainment in Punta Cana?

3 GRAMMAR FOCUS

Adverbs before adjectives

Punta Cana is **really** nice. It's a **really** nice place.
It's **fairly** expensive. It's a **fairly** expensive destination.
It's not **very** big. It's not a **very** big city.

New York is **too** noisy, and it's **too** crowded for me.

GRAMMAR PLUS *see page 142*

adverbs

too
extremely
very/really
pretty
fairly/somewhat

A Match the questions with the answers. Then practice the conversations with a partner.

1. What's Seoul like? Is it an interesting place? ______
2. Do you like your hometown? Why or why not? ______
3. What's Sydney like? I've never been there. ______
4. Have you ever been to São Paulo? ______
5. What's the weather like in Chicago? ______

a. Oh, really? It's beautiful and very clean. It has a great harbor and beautiful beaches.
b. Yes, I have. It's an extremely large and crowded place, but I love it. It has excellent restaurants.
c. It's really nice in the summer, but it's too cold for me in the winter.
d. Not really. It's too small, and it's really boring. That's why I moved away.
e. Yes. It has amazing shopping, and the people are pretty friendly.

Conjunctions

Los Angeles is a big city, **and** the weather is nice.
Boston is a big city, **but** it's not too big.
It's a big city. It's not too big, **though**.
It's a big city. It's not too big, **however**.

GRAMMAR PLUS *see page 142*

B Choose the correct conjunctions and rewrite the sentences.

1. Kyoto is very nice. Everyone is extremely friendly. (and / but)
   ____
2. The streets are crowded during the day. They're very quiet at night. (and / though)
   ____
3. The weather is nice. Summers get pretty hot. (and / however)
   ____
4. You can rent a bicycle. It's expensive. (and / but)
   ____
5. It's an amazing city. I love to go there. (and / however)
   ____

Kyoto, Japan

C **GROUP WORK** Describe three cities or towns in your country. State two positive features and one negative feature for each.

A: Singapore is very exciting and there are a lot of things to do, but it's too expensive.
B: The weather in Bogotá is . . .

4 LISTENING Describing hometowns

A Listen to Abby and Christopher talk about their hometowns. What do they say about them? Choose the correct words.

Abby's hometown	Christopher's hometown
a fairly / not very large town	a really / fairly stressful place
somewhat / extremely beautiful	pretty / too crowded
pretty / very cheap	not very / extremely clean
_______________ quiet	_______________ expensive

B Listen again. Write another adverb you hear them use to describe their hometowns.

5 WRITING A great place to live

A Write about interesting places for tourists to visit in your hometown.

Otavalo is a very interesting town in Ecuador. It's to the north of Quito. It has a fantastic market, and a lot of tourists go there to buy handmade art and crafts. The scenery around Otavalo is very pretty and . . .

B **PAIR WORK** Exchange papers and read each other's articles. What did you learn about your partner's hometown?

6 SNAPSHOT

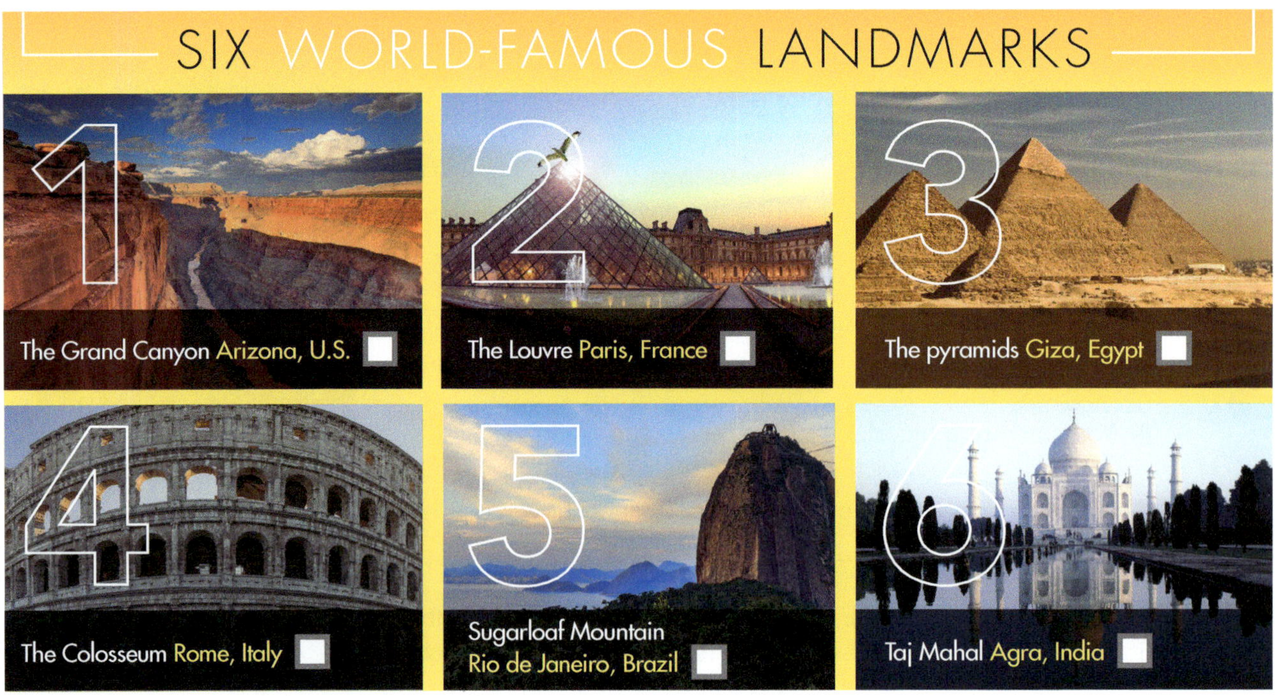

Which places would you like to visit? Why?
Put the places you would like to visit in order from most interesting (1) to least interesting (6).
Which interesting places around your country or the world have you already visited?
What three other places around the world would you like to visit? Why?

7 CONVERSATION What should I do there?

A Listen and practice.

JASON Can you tell me a little about Mexico City?

CLAUDIA Sure. What would you like to know?

JASON Well, I'm going to be there for a few days next month. What should I do there?

CLAUDIA Oh! You should definitely visit the National Museum of Anthropology. It's amazing.

JASON OK. It's on my list now! Anything else?

CLAUDIA You shouldn't miss the Diego Rivera murals. They're incredible. Oh, and you can walk around the historic center.

JASON That sounds perfect. And what about the food? What should I eat?

CLAUDIA You can't miss the street food. The tacos, barbecue, fruit . . . it's all delicious.

National Museum of Anthropology

Diego Rivera murals

B Listen to the rest of the conversation. Where is Jason from? What should you do there?

8 GRAMMAR FOCUS

Modal verbs *can* and *should*

What **can** I do in Mexico City?	What **should** I see there?
You **can** walk around the historic center.	You **should** visit the National Museum of Anthropology.
You **can't** miss the street food.	You **shouldn't** miss the Diego Rivera murals.

GRAMMAR PLUS *see page 142*

A Complete these conversations using *can*, *can't*, *should*, or *shouldn't*. Then practice with a partner.

1. **A:** I ______________ decide where to go on my vacation.
   B: You ______________ go to Morocco. It's my favorite place to visit.
2. **A:** I'm planning to go to Puerto Rico next year. When do you think I ______________ go?
   B: You ______________ go anytime. The weather is nice almost all year.
3. **A:** ______________ I rent a car when I arrive in New York? What do you recommend?
   B: No, you ______________ definitely use the subway. It's fast and not too expensive.
4. **A:** Where ______________ I get some nice jewelry in Istanbul?
   B: You ______________ miss the Grand Bazaar. It's the best place for bargains.
5. **A:** What ______________ I see from the Eiffel Tower?
   B: You ______________ see all of Paris, but in bad weather, you ______________ see anything.

B Write answers to these questions about your country. Then compare with a partner.

What time of year should you go there?
What are three things you can do there?
What can you do for free?
What shouldn't a visitor miss?

9 PRONUNCIATION *Can't and shouldn't*

A Listen and practice these statements. Notice how the *t* in **can't** and **shouldn't** is not strongly pronounced.

You can get a taxi easily.
You can'**t** get a taxi easily.
You should visit in the summer.
You shouldn'**t** visit in the summer.

Las Vegas, United States

B Listen to four sentences. Choose the modal verb you hear.

1. can / can't
2. should / shouldn't
3. can / can't
4. should / shouldn't

10 LISTENING Where should you go?

A Listen to speakers talk about three countries. Complete the chart.

Country	Largest city	What visitors should see or do
1. Japan		
2.		
3.		

B Listen again. What else do the speakers say about the countries?

11 SPEAKING What can visitors do there?

GROUP WORK Has anyone visited an interesting place in your country or in another country? Find out more about it. Start like this and ask questions like the ones below.

A: I visited Jeju Island once.
B: Really? What's the best time of year to visit?
A: Springtime is very nice. I went in May.
C: What's the weather like then?

What's the best time of year to visit?
What's the weather like then?
What should tourists see and do there?
What special foods can you eat?
What's the shopping like?
What things should people buy?
What else can visitors do there?

Jeju Island, South Korea

12 INTERCHANGE 11 Welcome to our city!

Make a guide to fun places in your city. Go to Interchange 11 on page 126.

13 READING

A Skim the emails. What city is famous for small plates of food? Where is a good place to ride your bike at night?

A big "Hello!" from . . .

New mail — **Barcelona, Spain** — Reply | Forward | ×

Barcelona is simply awesome! The city is famous for the architect Antoni Gaudí. I've seen a different Gaudí building every day. Gaudí designed some amazing places like the church *La Sagrada Familia*. Workers started building the church in 1882, but it isn't finished yet. Some people say it might be finished by 2030. I've also visited *Las Ramblas*, a street with great cafés. I've eaten delicious tapas every day. A *tapa* is a small plate of food. My friends and I usually order several tapas and share them. The weather is great! I think I came here at just the right time of the year.
Kathy

New mail — **Cartagena, Colombia** — Reply | Forward | ×

I've discovered that Cartagena has two different personalities. One is a lively city with fancy restaurants and crowded old plazas. And the other is a quiet and relaxing place with sandy beaches. If you come here, you should stay in the historic district – a walled area with great shopping, nightclubs, and restaurants. It has some wonderful old Spanish buildings. Last night I learned some salsa steps at an old dance club. Today, I went on a canoe tour of *La Ciénaga* mangrove forest.
Mike

New mail — **Bangkok, Thailand** — Reply | Forward | ×

Bangkok is the most exciting place I've ever visited. There's something for everyone. You can surf or swim with sharks. Or why not try out some extreme cycling at Peppermint Bike Park? The park has two great bike paths. You can ride your bike there until 10:00 at night. I ate the most delicious food in Bangkok, including the famous pad thai – a spicy noodle dish. At night, there are clubs, restaurants, cafés, and movie theaters to visit. It's impossible to be bored. I love it!
Jasmin

B Read the emails. Check (✓) the cities where you can do these things. Then complete the chart with examples from the emails.

Activity	Barcelona	Cartagena	Bangkok	Examples
1. swim with sharks	☐	☐	☐	
2. see a famous church	☐	☐	☐	
3. eat spicy food	☐	☐	☐	
4. go dancing	☐	☐	☐	
5. take a boat tour	☐	☐	☐	
6. eat small plates of local food	☐	☐	☐	

C **PAIR WORK** Which city is the most interesting to you? Why? Which other city or cities in the world would you like to visit? Why?

12 It's important to get rest.

- State health problems and give advice
- Ask for advice and give suggestions about health products

1 SNAPSHOT

Common Health Problems

☐ a headache

☐ a cough

☐ a cold

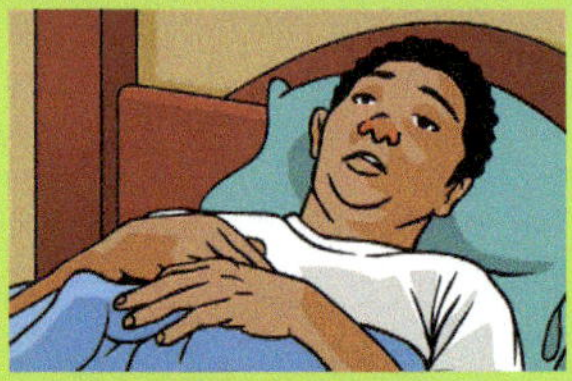

☐ the flu

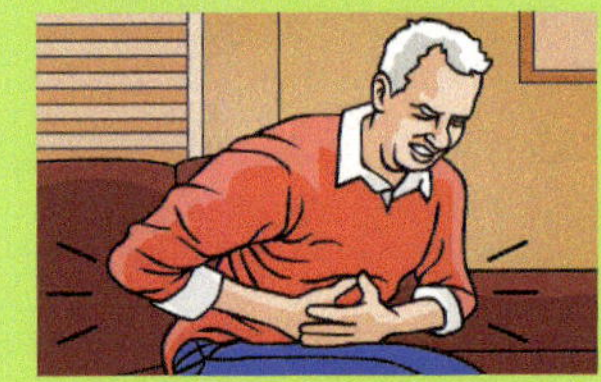

☐ a stomachache

☐ a backache

☐ sore muscles

☐ insomnia

How many times have you been sick in the past year?
Check (✓) the health problems you have had recently.
What do you do for the health problems you checked?

2 CONVERSATION It really works!

A Listen and practice.

Mila: Are you all right, Keith?
Keith: Not really. I don't feel so well. I have a terrible cold.
Mila: Oh, that's too bad. You shouldn't be at the gym, then.
Keith: Yeah, I know. But I need to run for an hour every day.
Mila: Not today, Keith! It's really important to get some rest.
Keith: Yeah, you're right. I should be in bed.
Mila: Well, yeah! And have you taken anything for your cold?
Keith: No, I haven't. What should I take?
Mila: Well, you know, pain medicine, lots of water. Sometimes it's helpful to drink garlic tea. Just chop up some garlic and boil it for a few minutes, then add lemon and honey. Try it! It really works!
Keith: Yuck! That sounds awful!

B Listen to advice from Keith's next-door neighbors. What do they suggest?

3 GRAMMAR FOCUS

Adjective + infinitive; noun + infinitive

What should you do for a cold?	It's **important**	**to get** some rest.
	It's sometimes **helpful**	**to drink** garlic tea.
	It's **a good idea**	**to take** some vitamin C.

GRAMMAR PLUS *see page 143*

A Look at these health problems. Choose several pieces of good advice for each problem.

Problems	**Advice**
1. a backache ______	**a.** drink lots of liquids
2. a bad headache ______	**b.** get some medicine
3. a burn ______	**c.** go to bed and rest
4. a cough ______	**d.** put it under cold water
5. a fever ______	**e.** put a heating pad on it
6. the flu ______	**f.** put some cream on it
7. a sore throat ______	**g.** see a dentist
8. a toothache ______	**h.** see a doctor
	i. take some pain medicine
	j. take some vitamin C

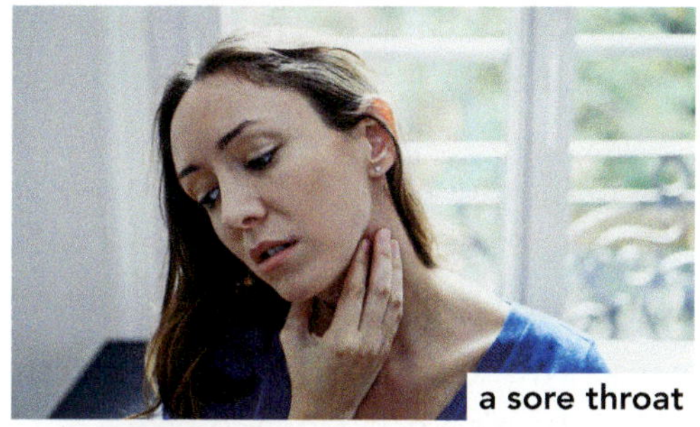
a sore throat

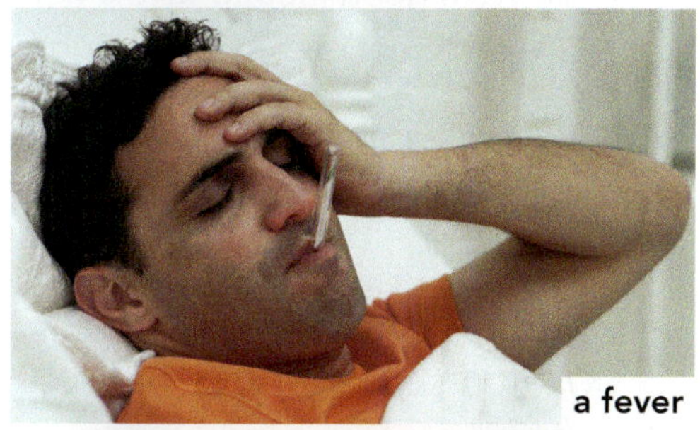
a fever

a toothache

a burn

B GROUP WORK Talk about the problems in part A and give advice. What other advice do you have?

A: What should you do for a backache?
B: It's a good idea to put a heating pad on it.
C: It's also important to see a doctor and . . .

C Write advice for these problems. (You will use this advice in Exercise 4.)

an earache **a cold** **a sunburn** **sore muscles**

For an earache, it's a good idea to . . .

4 PRONUNCIATION Reduction of *to*

A Listen and practice. In conversation, **to** is often reduced to /tə/.

A: What should you do for a toothache?
B: It's sometimes helpful **to** take some pain medicine. And it's important **to** see a dentist.

B PAIR WORK Look back at Exercise 3, part C. Ask for and give advice about each health problem. Pay attention to the pronunciation of **to**.

5 INTERCHANGE 12 What should I do?

Play a board game. Go to Interchange 12 on page 127.

6 DISCUSSION Good advice

A GROUP WORK Imagine these situations are true for you. Get three suggestions for each one from your partners.

I sometimes feel really stressed.
I need to study, but I can't concentrate.
I feel sick before every exam.
I forget about half the new words I learn.
I get nervous when I speak English to foreigners.
I get really hungry before I go to bed.

A: I sometimes feel really stressed. What should I do?
B: It's a good idea to take a hot bath.
C: It's sometimes helpful to go for a walk.

B CLASS ACTIVITY Have any of the above situations happened to you recently? Share what you did with the class.

7 WORD POWER Containers

A Use the words in the list to complete these expressions. Then compare with a partner. Sometimes more than one answer is correct.

bag	jar
bottle	pack
box	stick
can	tube

1. a ______________ of pain medicine
2. a ______________ of bandages
3. a ______________ of cough drops
4. a ______________ of deodorant
5. a ______________ of face cream
6. a ______________ of shaving cream
7. a ______________ of tissues
8. a ______________ of toothpaste

B PAIR WORK What is one more thing you can buy in each of the containers above?

"You can buy a bag of breath mints."

C PAIR WORK What are the five most useful items in your medicine cabinet?

8 CONVERSATION Can you suggest anything?

A Listen and practice.

Pharmacist: Hi. May I help you?

Mr. Peters: Yes, please. Could I have something for a backache? My muscles are really sore.

Pharmacist: Well, it's a good idea to use a heating pad. And why don't you try this cream? It works really well.

Mr. Peters: OK, I'll take one tube. Also, my wife has a bad cough. Can you suggest anything?

Pharmacist: She should try these cough drops.

Mr. Peters: Thanks! May I have a large bag? And what do you suggest for insomnia?

Pharmacist: Well, you could get a box of chamomile tea. Is it for you?

Mr. Peters: Yes, I can't sleep.

Pharmacist: A sore back and your wife's bad cough? I think I know why you can't sleep!

B Listen to the pharmacist talk to the next customer. What does the customer want?

9 GRAMMAR FOCUS

Modal verbs *can, could,* and *may* for requests; suggestions

Can/May I help you?	What do you suggest/have for a backache?
Can I have a bag of cough drops?	You could try this new cream.
Could I have something for a cough?	You should get a heating pad.
May I have a bottle of pain medicine?	Why don't you try these pills?

GRAMMAR PLUS *see page 143*

Choose the correct words. Then compare and practice with a partner.

1. **A:** **Can** / **Could** I help you?
   B: What do you **suggest** / **try** for dry skin?
   A: Why don't you **suggest** / **try** this lotion? It's excellent.
   B: OK. I'll take it.
2. **A:** **May** / **Do** I have something for itchy eyes?
   B: Sure. You **could** / **may** try a bottle of eyedrops.
3. **A:** Could I **suggest** / **have** a box of bandages, please?
   B: Here you are.
   A: And what do you **suggest** / **try** for insomnia?
   B: You **should** / **may** try this herbal tea. It's very relaxing.
   A: OK. Thanks.

10 LISTENING What's wrong?

Listen to four people talking about problems and giving advice. Write the problem and the advice.

	Problem	Advice
1. John		
2. Ashley		
3. Brandon		
4. Rachel		

11 ROLE PLAY Can I help you?

Student A: You are a customer in a drugstore. You need:

something for a backache
something for dry skin
something for the flu
something for low energy
something for sore feet
something for an upset stomach

Ask for some suggestions.

Student B: You are a pharmacist in a drugstore.
A customer needs some things.
Make some suggestions.

Change roles and try the role play again.

12 WRITING Reacting to a blog post

A Read this health and fitness blog post on how to avoid stress.

Home About Healthy living

Suggestions for a Relaxing Life

Tuesday, March 29 healthyandhappy

Can we avoid stress in our lives? What should we do to have a relaxing life? Everyone wants the answers to these questions. Well, we have a few suggestions:

- We should not work long hours or work on our days off.
- We should try to exercise three or four times a week.
- It's a good idea to buy only the things we really need.
- It's really important to have fun. Fun is the perfect remedy for stress!

B Now imagine you have your own blog. Write a post with your ideas on how to reduce stress and have a relaxing life. Think of an interesting name for your blog.

C **GROUP WORK** Exchange blog posts. Read your partners' blogs and write a suggestion at the bottom of each post. Then share the most interesting blog and suggestions with the class.

13 READING

A Skim the article. Then check the best description of the article.

☐ The article gives the author's opinion about the subject.
☐ The article gives information and facts.
☐ The article tells a story about a scientist.

Toothache?

Visit the rain forest!

acmella oleracea

A Nobody likes having a toothache, and not many people enjoy visiting the dentist's office. Exciting new research suggests that there is a different way to treat a toothache – one that doesn't need an appointment with a dentist.

B Scientists say that a very rare red and yellow plant from the Amazon rain forest could stop a toothache. It's more powerful than taking pain medicine, and it's more effective than most treatments you get in the dentist's chair. The plant, named *acmella oleracea,* has been used as a remedy for toothaches by the Keshwa Lamas, a Peruvian community, for many years.

C Dr. Françoise Barbira Freedman is an anthropologist – a scientist who studies humans. She learned about the plant 30 years ago on a trip to Peru. One day, she got a terrible toothache. The people in the village where she was living gave her the remedy and her pain disappeared.

D Now this amazing plant has been made into a gel. Many tests show that it really helps with the pain of toothaches and even helps babies who are getting their first teeth. To thank the Keshwa Lamas for this remedy, there is a plan to give some of the money from the gel back to the community. So it's good news for everyone.

B Read the article. Then answer these questions. Write the letter of the paragraph where you find the answers.

1. ______ When did Dr. Freedman learn about the plant?
2. ______ What has the plant been made into?
3. ______ What is the plant's scientific name?
4. ______ Who gave Dr. Freedman the remedy?
5. ______ What will be given back to the Keshwa Lamas?
6. ______ Where can you find the plant?

C **GROUP WORK** What are some other reasons why rain forests are important?

Units 11–12 Progress check

SELF-ASSESSMENT

How well can you do these things? Check (✓) the boxes.

I can . . .	Very well	OK	A little
Understand descriptions of towns and cities (Ex. 1)	☐	☐	☐
Get useful information about towns and cities (Ex. 1, 2)	☐	☐	☐
Describe towns and cities (Ex. 2)	☐	☐	☐
Ask for and make suggestions (Ex. 2, 3, 4)	☐	☐	☐
Ask and answer questions about experiences (Ex. 3, 4)	☐	☐	☐
Ask for and give advice about problems (Ex. 4)	☐	☐	☐

1 LISTENING So, you're from Hawaii?

A Listen to Megan talk about Honolulu. What does she say about these things? Complete the chart.

1. size of city ________	**3.** prices of things ________
2. weather ________	**4.** Waikiki Beach ________

B Write sentences comparing Honolulu with your hometown. Then discuss with a partner.

Honolulu isn't too big, but Seoul is really big.

2 ROLE PLAY My hometown

Student A: Imagine you are planning to visit Student B's hometown. Ask questions to learn more about the place. Use the questions in the box and your own ideas.

Student B: Answer Student A's questions about your hometown.

A: What's your hometown like?
B: It's very interesting, but it's crowded and polluted.

Change roles and try the role play again.

possible questions

What's your hometown like?
How big is it?
What's the weather like?
Is it expensive?
What should you see there?
What can you do there?

3 DISCUSSION Medicines and remedies

A **GROUP WORK** Write your suggestions for these common problems and then discuss your ideas in groups.

a stomachache

an insect bite

the hiccups

a nosebleed

For a stomachache, it's a good idea to . . .

A: What can you do for a stomachache?
B: I think it's helpful to drink herbal tea.
C: Yes. And it's a good idea to see a doctor.

B **GROUP WORK** What health problems do you visit a doctor for? go to a drugstore for? use a home remedy for? Ask for advice and remedies.

4 SPEAKING What's your advice?

A **GROUP WORK** Read these people's problems. Suggest advice for each problem. Then choose the best advice.

I'm visiting the United States. I'm staying with a family while I'm here. What small gifts can I get for them?

My co-worker always talks loudly to his friends during work hours. I can't concentrate! What can I do?

Our school wants to buy some new gym equipment. Can you suggest some good ways to raise money?

A: Why doesn't she give them some flowers? They're always nice.
B: That's a good idea. Or she could bring chocolates.
C: I think she should . . .

B **CLASS ACTIVITY** Share your group's advice for each problem with the class.

WHAT'S NEXT?

Look at your Self-assessment again. Do you need to review anything?

13 What would you like?

- ▸ Agree and disagree about food preferences
- ▸ Order food in a restaurant

1 SNAPSHOT

Favorite Foods

apple pie

☐ brought to North America from Europe in the 17th century

chocolate

☐ originally prepared as a drink by the Olmec people in Mexico over 3,000 years ago

french fries

☐ first made in Belgium around 1680

hamburger

☐ created around 1900 in the U.S. as a quick and inexpensive meal

ice-cream cone

☐ created at the 1904 World's Fair in the U.S. by a Syrian chef, Ernest Hamwi

pasta

☐ first written about in a Greek recipe from the 1st century CE

the sandwich

☐ named for the English Earl of Sandwich in the 1760s

sushi

☐ modern style sushi first made in Japan in the 1820s

What are these foods made of? Put the foods in order from your favorite (1) to your least favorite (8). What are three other foods you enjoy? Which have you eaten recently?

2 CONVERSATION I'm tired of shopping.

A Listen and practice.

Simon: Hey, do you want to get something to eat?
Kristin: Sure. I'm tired of shopping.
Simon: So am I. What do you think of Thai food?
Kristin: I love it, but I'm not really in the mood for it today.
Simon: Yeah. I'm not either, I guess. It's a bit spicy.
Kristin: What about Japanese food?
Simon: Fine by me! I love Japanese food.
Kristin: So do I. There's a great restaurant on the first floor. It's called Kyoto Garden.
Simon: Perfect. Let's go try it.

B Listen to the rest of the conversation. What do they decide to do after eating? Is there something they don't want to do?

3 GRAMMAR FOCUS

So, too, neither, either

	Agree	**Disagree**
I'**m** crazy about Italian food.	**So am** I./I **am**, **too**.	Oh, I'**m not**.
I **can** eat really spicy food.	**So can** I./I **can**, **too**.	Really? I **can't**.
I **like** Japanese food a lot.	**So do** I./I **do**, **too**.	Oh, I **don't (like it very much).**
I'**m not** in the mood for Indian food.	**Neither am** I./I'**m not either**.	Really? I **am**.
I **can't** stand fast food.	**Neither can** I./I **can't either**.	Oh, I **love** it!
I **don't like** salty food.	**Neither do** I./I **don't either**.	Oh, I **like** it a lot.

GRAMMAR PLUS *see page 144*

bland

delicious

greasy

healthy

rich

salty

spicy

A Write responses to show agreement with these statements. Then compare with a partner.

1. I'm not crazy about Italian food. ______________________
2. I can eat any kind of food. ______________________
3. I think Indian food is delicious. ______________________
4. I can't stand greasy food. ______________________
5. I don't like salty food. ______________________
6. I'm in the mood for something spicy. ______________________
7. I'm tired of fast food. ______________________
8. I don't enjoy rich food very much. ______________________
9. I always eat healthy food. ______________________
10. I can't eat bland food. ______________________

B **PAIR WORK** Take turns responding to the statements in part A again. Give your own opinion when responding.

C Write statements about these things. (You will use the statements in Exercise 4.)

1. two kinds of food you like
2. two kinds of food you can't stand
3. two kinds of food you would like to eat today

4 PRONUNCIATION Stress in responses

A Listen and practice. Notice how the last word of each response is stressed.

I do, too.	So do I.	I don't either.	Neither do I.
I am, too.	So am I.	I'm not either.	Neither am I.
I can, too.	So can I.	I can't either.	Neither can I.

B **PAIR WORK** Read and respond to the statements your partner wrote for Exercise 3, part C. Pay attention to the stress in your responses.

5 WORD POWER Food categories

A Complete the chart. Then add one more word to each category.

bread	fish	mangoes	peas	shrimp
chicken	grapes	octopus	potatoes	strawberries
corn	lamb	pasta	rice	turkey

Fruit	Vegetables	Grains	Meat	Seafood

B **GROUP WORK** What's your favorite food in each category? Are there any you haven't tried?

6 CONVERSATION May I take your order?

A Listen and practice.

Server: May I take your order?

Customer: Yes, please. I'd like the veggie burger.

Server: All right. And would you like soup or salad with your burger?

Customer: What's the soup of the day?

Server: It's chicken soup. We also have cream of potato soup and onion soup.

Customer: I'll have the onion soup, please.

Server: And would you like anything to drink?

Customer: Yes, I'd like a lemonade, please.

B Listen to the server talk to the next customer. What does he order?

7 GRAMMAR FOCUS

Modal verbs *would* and *will* for requests

What **would** you **like**?	I'**d like** the veggie burger. I'**ll have** a mango salad.	**Contractions** I'**ll** = I will I'**d** = I would
What kind of soup **would** you **like**?	I'**d like** onion soup, please. I'**ll have** the soup of the day.	
What **would** you **like** to drink?	I'**d like** a lemonade. I'**ll have** a large orange juice.	
Would you **like** anything else?	Yes, please. I'**d like** some coffee. That's all, thanks.	

GRAMMAR PLUS *see page 144*

Complete this conversation. Then practice with a partner.

Server: What ____________ you like to order?
Customer: I ____________ have the spicy fish.
Server: ____________ you like salad or potatoes?
Customer: I ____________ like potatoes, please.
Server: OK. And ____________ you like anything to drink?
Customer: I ____________ just have a glass of water.
Server: Would you ____________ anything else?
Customer: No, that's all for now, thanks.

Later

Server: Would you ____________ dessert?
Customer: Yes, I ____________ like ice cream.
Server: What flavor ____________ you like?
Customer: Hmm. I ____________ have mint chocolate chip, please.

8 ROLE PLAY At a coffee shop

Student A: You are a customer at a coffee shop. Order what you want for lunch.
Student B: You are the server. Take your customer's order.

TODAY'S LUNCH SPECIALS

Cheeseburger with onion rings
Spicy shrimp and rice
Chicken salad sandwich
Lamb curry and potatoes
Sushi plate with miso soup
Vegetarian pizza and salad

Drinks

Coffee
Tea
Soda
Fresh juice
Sparkling water

Desserts

Ice cream
Chocolate cake
Lemon pie
Fresh fruit salad

Change roles and try the role play again.

9 LISTENING Working late

A Steven and Sarah are working late. Listen as their boss asks what they would like for dinner. What do they order? Fill in their choices.

Steven	Sarah
______________ pizza	______________ pizza
Salad with ______________	Salad with ______________ dressing
Drink: ______________ with ______________	Drink: ______________ with ______________
Dessert: a piece of ______________	Dessert: a slice of ______________

B Listen to their conversation after the food arrives. Choose the two items that are missing from the order.

10 INTERCHANGE 13 Planning a food festival

Create a menu to offer at a food festival. Go to Interchange 13 on page 128.

11 WRITING A restaurant review

A Have you eaten out recently? Write a review of a restaurant, café, or food truck. Choose at least five questions from the list. Answer these questions and add ideas of your own.

What's the name of the place?
When did you go there?
What time did you go?
Who did you go with?
What did you have to eat?
What did you have to drink?
Did you order dessert?
What did you like about the place?
What didn't you like about it?
Would you recommend it? Why? Why not?

B **GROUP WORK** Take turns reading your reviews. Which place would you like to try?

Last Saturday, my sister and I tried Burger To Go, a new restaurant in our town. I had a classic cheeseburger and fries. The burger wasn't very big, but it was delicious. The fries were hot and crispy but a little too salty. For dessert, I had apple pie. It wasn't bad, but I've had better. I would recommend Burger To Go for their burgers and their very friendly service. I hope they improve with time!
– Emilia

12 READING

A Scan the article. In which country do people usually leave a 15–20% tip on food? In which country is tipping unnecessary?

TO TIP OR NOT TO TIP?

WHAT'S A TIP?

The verb *to tip* means to give money, and the noun *tip* is the money that you give to someone. It's a slang word from Old English. Around the world, many people give tips to people who provide a service for them. It's a way of saying thank you. But did you know that tipping customs around the world *vary* a lot?

WHO AND WHERE TO TIP

In some countries, like the United States, it's common to give a tip in a lot of different places. Almost everybody gives tips to servers in restaurants and cafés. Servers *rely on* those tips to add to the low *wages* they get paid for their jobs. People also tip taxi drivers and hairstylists. If an airport worker or a hotel bellhop helps you with a heavy suitcase, you tip them as well. In Japan, though, it's a very different story. In Japan, tipping isn't part of the culture, so it rarely happens. In fact, a tip might be *confusing* to the server. And in France, a "service charge" is included on all restaurant checks, so in fact, you've already tipped your server.

HOW MUCH TO TIP?

The amount people tip in the United States varies between 15 and 20% on restaurant checks. So, for example, if a restaurant total is $40, people give the server around $6–8. That seems like a lot of money for some visitors who come from countries where tipping isn't *customary*. According to one news source, the average tip in a New York restaurant is 19.1% of the total, but in London it's 11.8%. That's a big difference.

WHO'S THE BEST TIPPER?

A millionaire named Benjamin Olewine probably wins the prize for giving the world's most *generous* tip. Mr. Olewine paid for his server's nursing school fees as a tip! The waitress, Melissa, was working in a restaurant to save money for school. One day, she served breakfast to Mr. Olewine. The check was $3.45. The tip was more than $20,000!

B Read the article. Find the words in italics, then check (✓) the correct meaning of each word.

1. *vary* ☐ change ☐ stay the same
2. *rely on* ☐ ask for ☐ need
3. *wages* ☐ regular pay for a job ☐ tips received for a job
4. *confusing* ☐ unnecessary ☐ difficult to understand
5. *customary* ☐ usual ☐ unusual
6. *generous* ☐ very rich ☐ giving more than enough

C Check (✓) the statements that describe correct tipping behavior. For the items you don't check, what is acceptable?

☐ **1.** You're eating at a restaurant in London. You leave a 25% tip.
☐ **2.** You give your New York server a 15% tip.
☐ **3.** You give a large tip after your meal in Tokyo.
☐ **4.** Your bellhop in Chicago helps you carry your suitcase. You give him a tip.
☐ **5.** You pay your check in Paris and don't leave a tip.

D **GROUP WORK** Is tipping customary in your country? If it is, who do you tip and how much? If it isn't, what do you think about tipping?

14 It's the coldest city!

- Describe and compare different places in the world
- Describe temperatures, distances, and measurements

1 WORD POWER Places around the world

A Match the words from the list to the letters in the picture. Then compare with a partner.

1. beach ______
2. desert ______
3. forest ______
4. hill ______
5. island ______
6. lake ______
7. mountain ______
8. ocean ______
9. river ______
10. valley ______
11. volcano ______
12. waterfall ______

B **PAIR WORK** What other geography words can you think of? Do you see any of these places in the picture above?

C **GROUP WORK** Try to think of famous examples for each item in part A.

A: A famous beach is Shirahama Beach in Japan.
B: And the Sahara is a famous . . .

2 CONVERSATION I love quizzes!

A Listen and practice.

Claire: This is one of the best airline magazines I've ever read. Oh, look! A quiz! "Our world – How much do you know?"
Steve: Oh, I love quizzes! Ask me the questions.
Claire: Sure. First question: Which country is larger, Mexico or Australia?
Steve: I know. Australia is larger than Mexico.
Claire: OK, next. What's the longest river in the world?
Steve: That's easy. It's the Nile!
Claire: All right. Here's a hard one. Which country is more crowded, Malta or England?
Steve: I'm not sure. I think Malta is more crowded.
Claire: Really? OK, one more. Which city is the most expensive: Hong Kong, London, or Paris?
Steve: Oh, that's easy. Paris is the most expensive.

B Listen to the rest of the conversation. How many questions did Steve get right?

3 GRAMMAR FOCUS

Comparisons with adjectives

Which country is **larger**, Australia or Mexico?
Australia is **larger than** Mexico.

Which country is **the largest** in the world?
Russia is **the largest** country.

Which is **more crowded**? Malta or England?
Malta is **more crowded than** England.
Malta is **the most crowded** country in Europe.

Adjective	Comparative	Superlative
long	longer	the longest
large	larger	the largest
dry	drier	the driest
big	bigger	the biggest
beautiful	more beautiful	the most beautiful
crowded	more crowded	the most crowded
expensive	more expensive	the most expensive
good	better	the best
bad	worse	the worst

GRAMMAR PLUS *see page 145*

A Complete questions 1 to 4 with comparatives and questions 5 to 8 with superlatives. Then ask and answer the questions.

1. Which country is ______________, Monaco or Vatican City? (small)
2. Which waterfall is ______________, Niagara Falls or Victoria Falls? (high)
3. Which city is ______________, Hong Kong or Cairo? (crowded)
4. Which lake is ______________, Lake Michigan or Lake Baikal? (large)
5. Which is ______________: Mount Aconcagua, Mount Everest, or Mount Fuji? (high)
6. What is ______________ river in the Americas, the Mississippi, the Colorado, or the Amazon? (long)
7. Which city is ______________: London, Tokyo, or Moscow? (expensive)
8. What is ______________ ocean in the world, the Pacific, the Atlantic, or the Arctic? (deep)

B **CLASS ACTIVITY** Write four questions like those in part A about your country or other countries. Then ask your classmates the questions.

4 PRONUNCIATION Questions of choice

A Listen and practice. Notice how the intonation in questions of choice drops, then rises, and then drops again.

Which city is more crowded, Hong Kong or Cairo?

Which city is the most expensive: London, Tokyo, or Moscow?

B **PAIR WORK** Take turns asking these questions. Pay attention to your intonation. Do you know the answers?

Which desert is bigger, the Gobi or the Atacama?
Which city is higher, Bogotá or La Paz?
Which ocean is the smallest: the Arctic, the Indian, or the Atlantic?
Which mountains are the highest: the Andes, the Rockies, or the Himalayas?

5 SPEAKING Travelers' tips

GROUP WORK Imagine these people are planning to visit your country. What would they enjoy doing? Agree on a recommendation for each person.

Jana

"I like all kinds of outdoor activities, especially hiking and bike riding. I can't stand crowded and polluted cities."

Neil

"I enjoy visiting museums, trying local food, and shopping at small stores. I don't like boring tourist places."

Sammie

"I love nightlife. My favorite activity is going dancing and meeting new people! I really don't like small towns."

6 LISTENING Quiz Show!

Listen to three people on a TV quiz show. Check (✓) the correct answers.

1.	☐ the Eiffel Tower	☐ the Statue of Liberty	☐ the Panama Canal
2.	☐ Victoria Falls	☐ Niagara Falls	☐ Angel Falls
3.	☐ gold	☐ butter	☐ all
4.	☐ the Arctic Ocean	☐ the Southern Ocean	☐ the Indian Ocean
5.	☐ São Paulo	☐ Mexico City	☐ Seoul
6.	☐ Africa	☐ Antarctica	☐ Australia

7 INTERCHANGE 14 How much do you know?

You probably know more than you think! Take a quiz. Go to Interchange 14 on page 129.

8 SNAPSHOT

8 Surprising Facts

1 The hottest place in the world is Death Valley, California. The temperature there has reached 134°F (56.7°C).

2 Antarctica is the largest desert on Earth. It is 5.4 million square miles (14 million square kilometers). It's also the coldest, windiest continent.

3 *NCIS* is the world's most watched TV show. Over 55 million people across the world have watched it.

4 The largest cat in the world is the Siberian tiger. At 700 pounds (320 kilos), it is bigger than a lion.

5 France is the most popular country to visit. It gets over 80 million visitors a year.

6 The highest price for a car at an auction was just over $38 million for a 1962 Ferrari. The auction happened in 2014.

7 The best-selling music album of all time is Michael Jackson's *Thriller*. The 1982 album has sold around 65 million copies.

8 The planet in our Solar System with the most moons, 67 total, is Jupiter. The largest one, Ganymede, is the ninth largest object in the Solar System.

Which facts do you find surprising? Why?
What are some facts about your country? What's the tallest building? the busiest airport? the most popular city to visit?

9 CONVERSATION That's freezing!

A Listen and practice.

Alberto: Hi, Lily. You're from Canada, right? I'm going to Toronto in January.
Lily: Actually, I'm from the U.S., but I went to school in Toronto. Winter there can be pretty cold.
Alberto: How cold is it on average?
Lily: Um, I think the average in January is around 20° or maybe 25°.
Alberto: Twenty-five degrees? But that's warm!
Lily: Twenty-five degrees Fahrenheit. That's about . . . minus 3 or 4 Celsius.
Alberto: Minus 3 or 4? That's freezing!
Lily: Oh, come on, that's not *so* cold, at least not where I'm from.
Alberto: Really? Where are you from?
Lily: Well, I live in Fairbanks, Alaska, around 3,000 miles from Toronto. That's . . . let me check on my phone . . . Yes, that's about 4,800 kilometers.
Alberto: Wow. . . . So, is it colder than Toronto?
Lily: It's much colder than Toronto. It's the coldest city in the United States!

B Listen to the rest of the conversation. Is Fairbanks a small town? What else does Lily say about it?

10 GRAMMAR FOCUS

Questions with *how*

How cold is Toronto in the winter?	It gets down to minus 25° Celsius.	(-13° Fahrenheit)
How hot is Fairbanks in the summer?	It gets up to about 20° Celsius.	(68° Fahrenheit)
How far is Toronto from Fairbanks?	It's about 4,800 kilometers.	(3,000 miles)
How big is Seoul?	It's 605 square kilometers.	(233.6 square miles)
How high is Mount Everest?	It's 8,848 meters **high**.	(29,028 feet)
How long is the Mississippi River?	It's about 3,700 kilometers **long.**	(2,300 miles)
How deep is the Grand Canyon?	It's about 1,828 meters **deep**.	(6,000 feet)

GRAMMAR PLUS *see page 145*

A Write the questions to these answers. Then practice with a partner.

1. **A:** ____?
   B: Niagara Falls is 52 meters (170 feet) high.
2. **A:** ____?
   B: California is about 423,970 square kilometers (163,670 square miles).
3. **A:** ____?
   B: The Nile is 6,670 kilometers (4,145 miles) long.
4. **A:** ____?
   B: Osaka is about 400 kilometers (250 miles) from Tokyo.
5. **A:** ____?
   B: Mexico City gets up to about 28° Celsius (82° Fahrenheit) in the summer.

B **GROUP WORK** Think of five questions with *how* about places in your country or other countries you know. Ask and answer your questions.

11 WRITING An article about a place

A Write an article about a place in your country or in another country that you think tourists would like to visit. Describe a place from the list.

a beach
a desert
an island
a lake
a mountain
a river
a volcano
a waterfall

B **PAIR WORK** Read your partner's article. Ask questions to get more information.

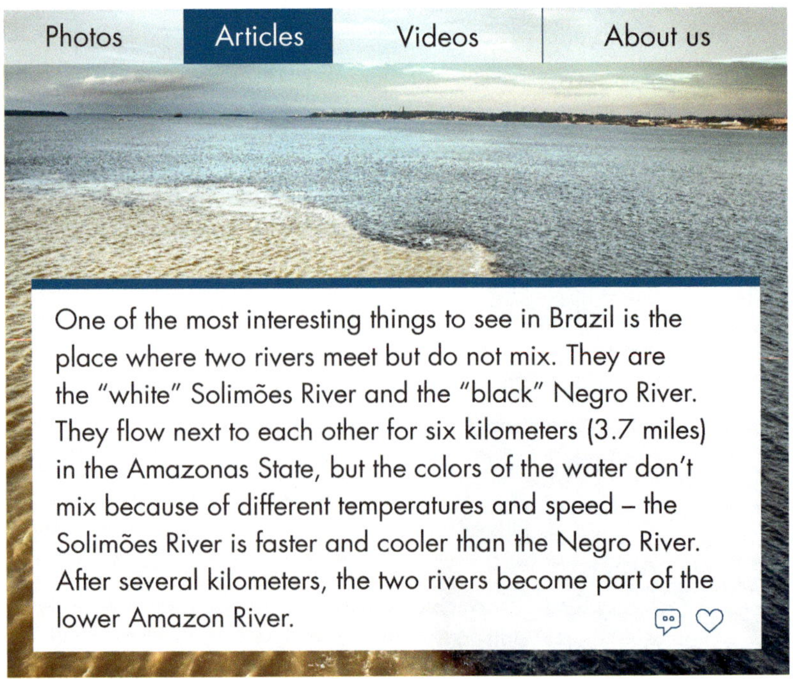

12 READING

A Look at the title of the article and the pictures. Why do you think these places are so clean?

Earth's Cleanest Places

Lake Vostok, Antarctica

About four kilometers (2.5 miles) under a large area of ice in Antarctica, there's a lake named Lake Vostok. It covers 15,690 square kilometers (6,058 square miles) and is 800 meters (2,625 feet) deep in some places. Lake Vostok is prehistoric – millions of years old – but until 1956, no one even knew it existed. It's a fresh water lake, and it has been hidden from sunlight for 15 million years. What this means is that the water is some of the cleanest, purest water on Earth.

Cape Grim, Australia

We all know that air pollution is a problem all around the world, so where do you go if you want really clean air? Well, Cape Grim in Tasmania, Australia is probably the best idea. Cape Grim has some of the cleanest air on Earth. Cape Grim also has beautiful, clean water. Why is this? Wind! Special winds called "The Roaring Forties" cross the Southern Ocean, bringing with them wonderfully clean water and air. In fact, in Cape Grim, people are allowed to put rain water into bottles and sell it. That's how clean it is!

Singapore

The tiny island of Singapore has a population of about 5.7 million people. It also has very strict rules about the way its people behave. Singapore is one of the cleanest cities on the planet because of these rules. People are not allowed to chew gum unless it's from a doctor, and all used chewing gum has to go in a trash can. That means that you don't find gum on the sidewalks. In fact, no one drops trash in the street.There are big fines for people who don't respect the rules, but most people are happy to keep their city clean and healthy.

B Read the article. What is the main goal of the article? Check (✓) the correct answer.

☐ to entertain people ☐ to inform people ☐ to persuade people to do something

C Read the article and answer the questions.

1. When did people discover Lake Vostok? ______
2. How long has Lake Vostok been hidden? ______
3. What two things is Cape Grim famous for? ______
4. What's the main reason that Cape Grim is so clean? ______
5. About how many people live in Singapore? ______
6. What happens when people break the rules in Singapore? ______

D **GROUP WORK** What do you think is the cleanest place in your country? Why is it so clean? How would you describe it to a friend?

Units 13–14 Progress check

SELF-ASSESSMENT

How well can you do these things? Check (✓) the boxes.

I can . . .	Very well	OK	A little
Say what I like and dislike (Ex. 1)	☐	☐	☐
Agree and disagree with other people (Ex. 1)	☐	☐	☐
Understand a variety of questions in a restaurant (Ex. 2)	☐	☐	☐
Order a meal in a restaurant (Ex. 3)	☐	☐	☐
Describe and compare things, people, and places (Ex. 4, 5)	☐	☐	☐
Ask questions about distances and measurements (Ex. 5)	☐	☐	☐

1 SPEAKING Survey: food preferences

A Answer these questions. Write your responses under the column "My answers." Then add one more question to the chart.

	My answers	Classmate's name
What food are you crazy about?		
What food can't you stand?		
Do you like vegetarian food?		
Can you eat very spicy food?		
How often do you go out to eat?		
What restaurant do you like a lot?		
______________________		

B CLASS ACTIVITY Go around the class. Find someone who has the same opinions or habits.

A: I'm crazy about Japanese food.
B: I am, too./So am I. OR Oh, I'm not. I'm crazy about . . .

2 LISTENING In a restaurant

Listen to six requests in a restaurant. Check (✓) the best response.

1. ☐ Yes. This way, please.
   ☐ Yes, please.
2. ☐ No, I don't.
   ☐ Yes, I'll have tea, please.
3. ☐ I'd like the fish, please.
   ☐ Yes, I would.
4. ☐ I'll have a green salad.
   ☐ Italian, please.
5. ☐ Broccoli, please.
   ☐ Yes, I would.
6. ☐ Yes, I'd like more water.
   ☐ No, I don't think so.

3 ROLE PLAY May I take your order?

Student A: Imagine you are a server and Student B is a customer. Take his or her order and write it on the check.

Student B: Imagine you are a hungry customer at any restaurant you choose. Student A is a server. Order a meal.

Change roles and try the role play again.

....
....
....
....
....
THANK YOU TOTAL: ....

4 SPEAKING Your hometown quiz

A **PAIR WORK** Write down six facts about your town or city using comparatives or superlatives. Then write six Wh-questions based on your facts.

1. The longest street is Independence Street.
What's the longest street in our city?

B **GROUP WORK** Join another pair. Take turns asking the other pair your questions. How many can they answer correctly?

5 GAME What's the question?

A Think of three statements that can be answered with *how* questions or Wh-questions with comparatives and superlatives. Write each statement on a separate card.

June and July are the coldest months in our city.

The Atacama is drier than the Sahara.

It's about two kilometers from my house to the school.

B **CLASS ACTIVITY** Divide into Teams A and B. Shuffle the cards together. One student from Team A picks a card and reads it to a student from Team B. That student tries to make a question for it.

A: The Atacama is drier than the Sahara.
B: Which desert is drier, the Atacama or the Sahara?

Keep score. The team with the most correct questions wins.

WHAT'S NEXT?

Look at your Self-assessment again. Do you need to review anything?

15 What are you doing later?

- Discuss future activities and plans
- Give messages

1 SNAPSHOT

HOW TO DECLINE AN INVITATION POLITELY

A friend has invited you to go out, but you can't make it. Follow our advice and learn how you can decline an invitation politely and keep your friend.

To thank your friend, you can say:
"Thanks so much for asking me. It sounds like a lot of fun."
"Thanks so much for the invite."

To apologize and explain why you can't accept, you can say:
"Sorry, but I already have plans."
"Sorry, but I have something else going on that day."
"I'm so sorry, but I can't make it. I'm really busy these days."

To offer another time to do something together, you can say:
"This week is crazy, but let's shoot for next week."
"Maybe another time? I'm free next week."
"Can I take a rain check?"

Do you feel comfortable declining friends' invitations? Why? Why not?
What polite excuses have you used? Which are effective? Which are not?
What is the best tip, in your opinion? Why?

2 CONVERSATION Are you doing anything tomorrow?

A Listen and practice.

Alicia: Hey, Mike, what are you doing tonight? Do you want to go see the new photo exhibit?
Mike: Thanks so much for asking me, but I can't. I'm going to have dinner with my parents.
Alicia: Oh, well, maybe some other time.
Mike: Are you doing anything tomorrow? We could go then.
Alicia: Tomorrow sounds fine. I have class until four.
Mike: So let's go around five.
Alicia: OK. Afterward, maybe we can get some dinner.
Mike: Sounds great.

B Listen to the rest of the conversation. Where are Alicia and Mike going to have dinner? Who are they going to meet for dinner?

3 GRAMMAR FOCUS

Future with present continuous and *be going to*

With present continuous	With *be going to* + verb	Time expressions
What **are** you **doing** tonight?	What **is** she **going to do** tomorrow?	tonight
I**'m going** to a party.	She**'s going to see a play.**	tomorrow
Are you **doing** anything tomorrow?	**Are** they **going to see** the photo exhibit?	on Friday
No, I**'m** not (**doing** anything).	Yes, they **are** (**going to see** it).	this weekend
		next week

GRAMMAR PLUS *see page 146*

A Complete the invitations in column A with the present continuous used as future. Complete the responses in column B with *be going to*.

A

1. What ______________ you ______________ (do) tonight? Would you like to go out?
2. ______________ you ______________ (do) anything on Friday night? Do you want to see a movie?
3. We ______________ (have) friends over for a barbecue on Sunday. Would you and your parents like to come?
4. ______________ you ______________ (stay) in town next weekend? Do you want to go for a hike?

B

a. I ______________ (be) here on Saturday, but not Sunday. Let's try to go on Saturday.
b. Well, my father ______________ (visit) my brother at college. But my mother and I ______________ (be) home. We'd love to come!
c. Sorry, I can't. I ______________ (work) late tonight. How about tomorrow night?
d. Can we go to a late show? I ______________ (stay) at the office till 7:00.

B Match the invitations in column A with the responses in column B. Then practice with a partner.

4 WORD POWER Free-time activities and events

A Complete the chart with words and phrases from the list. Then add one more example to each category.

a rock concert	a barbecue	a wedding	a hip-hop dance performance
a soccer game	a film festival	a musical	a video game tournament
a birthday party	a class reunion	a car race	a baseball game

Sports and games	Friends and family	Art and performances

B **PAIR WORK** Are you going to do any of the activities in part A? When are you doing them? Talk with a partner.

5 ROLE PLAY Accept or refuse?

Student A: Choose an activity from Exercise 4 and invite a partner to go with you. Be ready to say where and when the activity is.

A: So, are you doing anything on . . . ? Would you like to . . . ?

Student B: Your partner invites you out. Either accept the invitation and ask for more information or say you can't go and give an excuse.

Accept	**Refuse**
B: OK. That sounds fun. Where is it?	**B:** Oh, I'm sorry, I can't. I'm . . .

Change roles and try the role play again.

6 INTERCHANGE 15 Weekend plans

Find out what your classmates are going to do this weekend. Go to Interchange 15 on page 130.

7 CONVERSATION Can I take a message?

A Listen and practice.

CAITLIN Hello?

JAKE Hi, Caitlin. It's Jake. Are you busy?

CAITLIN No, I'm having coffee with Brittney. Where are you? Class is going to start soon.

JAKE That's the problem. I don't think I'm going to make it tonight.

CAITLIN Why not? What's the matter?

JAKE My bus is stuck in traffic. Nobody is moving.

CAITLIN Oh, no! What are you going to do?

JAKE I don't know. Could you tell Mr. Eaton that I'm going to miss class?

CAITLIN No problem. I'll give him the message.

JAKE Oh, and could you ask Brittney to take pictures of the whiteboard for me?

CAITLIN Sure. But I can take the pictures.

JAKE Um, thanks, but the last time you took a picture of the board all I could see was the wall!

B Listen to three other phone calls. Write the callers' names.

8 GRAMMAR FOCUS

Formal and informal messages with *tell* and *ask*

Statements	Messages with a statement: *tell*	
I'm going to miss class tonight.	(Please) **Tell him (that)** I'm going to miss class. **Could you tell him (that)** I'm going to miss class? **Would you tell him (that)** I'm going to miss class?	informal ↓ formal
Requests	**Messages with a request: *ask***	
Could she take a picture of the board?	(Please) **Ask her** to take a picture of the board. **Could you ask her** to take a picture of the board? **Would you ask her** to take a picture of the board?	informal ↓ formal

GRAMMAR PLUS *see page 146*

A Unscramble these messages. Then compare with a partner.

1. tell / that / is / please / Haru / the barbecue / on Saturday
   ______________________________.
2. call me / at / 4:00 / you / Caitlin / could /ask / to
   ______________________________?
3. is / that / Mia / tonight / could / you / the dance performance / tell
   ______________________________?
4. tell / is / Casey / in the park / would / you / that / the picnic
   ______________________________?
5. meet me / to / you / would / Maika / ask / at the stadium
   ______________________________?
6. ask / to the rock concert / please / bring / Garrett / to / the tickets
   ______________________________.

B **PAIR WORK** Imagine that you are far from school and cannot come to class. "Call" your partner and ask him or her to give a message to your teacher and to one of the students in your group.

A: Could you tell Ms. Clark that . . . And could you ask Joel to . . .

9 WRITING Text message requests

A **PAIR WORK** "Text" your partner. Write messages to each other with requests for your classmates. Write as many messages as you can in three minutes.

> A: Hi, Sandra. Would you ask Marcella to have dinner with us after class?
> B: OK, Chris. And could you tell Jules that we have a test tomorrow?

B **CLASS ACTIVITY** Give the messages to your classmates.

A: Hi, Jules. I have a message from Sandra. We have a test tomorrow.

B: Hi, Marcella. I have a message from Chris. Would you like to have dinner with us after class?

10 PRONUNCIATION Reduction of *could you* and *would you*

A Listen and practice. Notice how **could you** and **would you** are reduced in conversation.

[cʊdʒə]
Could you tell him I'm going to miss class?

[wʊdʒə]
Would you ask him to call me after class?

B PAIR WORK Practice these questions with reduced forms.

Could you tell them I'm in bed with a cold?
Would you ask her to be on time?
Could you ask her to return my dictionary?
Would you tell him there's a food festival tomorrow?

11 LISTENING I'm going to be late.

Listen to four people leaving messages. Who is the message from? Who is it for? What is the message? Complete the chart.

1
Message from: ____________________
Message for: ____________________
Message: ____________________
____

2
Message from: ____________________
Message for: ____________________
Message: ____________________
____

3
Message from: ____________________
Message for: ____________________
Message: ____________________
____

4
Message from: ____________________
Message for: ____________________
Message: ____________________
____

12 ROLE PLAY Who's calling?

Student A: You have a computer repair store. A client, Sophie Green, has left her laptop at your store. Call her to tell her this:

The computer needs a new motherboard. It's going to cost $250.
She can buy a used motherboard for $90. Could she please call you before 5:00?

Student B: Someone calls for your mother, Sophie Green. She isn't at home. Take a message for her.

Change roles and try another role play.

Student A: You are a receptionist at Techniware Industries. Someone calls for your boss, Mr. Yun. He isn't in. Take a message for him.

Student B: Call Mr. Yun at Techniware Industries to tell him this:

You can't make your lunch meeting at 12:00 next Wednesday. You would like to meet at 12:30 at the same place instead. Could he please call you to arrange the new time?

useful expressions

Caller
May I speak to . . . ?
Can I leave a message?

Receiver
Sorry, but . . . isn't here.
Can I take a message?
I'll give him/her the message.

13 READING

A Scan the article. Why did some people go to the wrong address?

Home | News | Technology | Lifestyle | Fashion | Politics | Food

Cell Phone Trouble!

Have you ever had an embarrassing time because of your cell phone? If you have, you're not alone. Check out this selection of cell phone "accidents."

Security cameras in a fancy hotel captured a video of a well-dressed woman, about 30 years old, texting on her phone. There's nothing unusual about that, is there? Well, yes, this time there is. The woman was so busy on her phone that she walked right into a pool of water in the hotel lobby . . . fully dressed! Nobody knows who the woman is or where the watery adventure happened, but almost half a million people have watched the video on the Internet!

A New Yorker was riding the subway home from work one evening. He was very excited by the video game he was playing on his smartphone. When he won the game, he threw his arms in the air in excitement . . . At that moment, the subway doors opened to let people on and off the train. The problem is that the man threw his phone right out of the subway car and on to the tracks below. Oops! No more video games for a while!

A lot of people are so busy looking at their smartphones that they often walk into lampposts and hurt themselves. The problem is so big that Brick Lane in London is now a "safe text" zone. Every lamppost in the street is covered in soft padding just in case somebody walks into it.

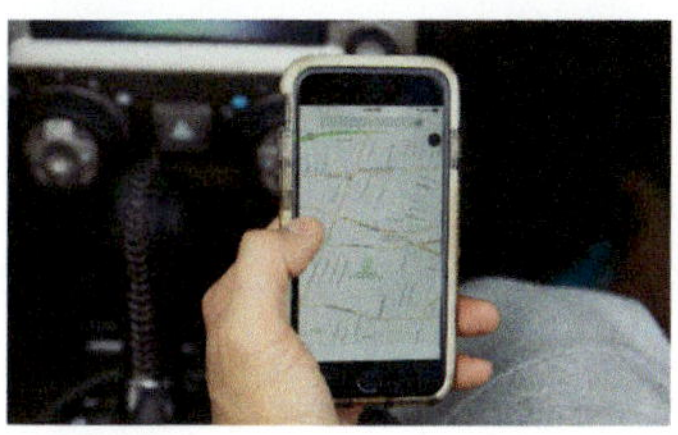

Most of us use map apps on our phones to get to the places we want to go. But sometimes, these apps get a little confused. A demolition company (a company that tears down buildings) used a map app to find a house. So far so good, right? Well, no. The map led the workers to the wrong house, a house one block away from the correct house in a town in Texas. The workers tore the house down. Imagine the owner's reaction when she arrived back home later that day!

B Read the article. Which advice best summarizes the article?

1. London is a great place to visit if you like using cell phones.
2. Be careful when you use your cell phone.
3. Lampposts and water are extremely dangerous.

C Check the facts that are mentioned in the article.

- ☐ **1.** A woman on a subway fell into some water while she was using her phone.
- ☐ **2.** Many people have watched a video of a woman falling into water.
- ☐ **3.** A man on a subway lost his phone.
- ☐ **4.** The man on the subway didn't like the video game he was playing.
- ☐ **5.** London has an area where you can text more safely.
- ☐ **6.** Every lamppost in London is padded.
- ☐ **7.** A demolition company tore down someone's home.
- ☐ **8.** The torn down building was in Texas.

D **PAIR WORK** Have you ever had a cell phone "accident?" What happened? What advice about cell phone safety would you give to a child?

16 How have you changed?

- ▸ Describe life changes
- ▸ Describe plans for the future

1 SNAPSHOT

LIFE-CHANGING EXPERIENCES

Change schools	Graduate from college	Fall in love
Move to a new house	Get a job	Get married
Turn 18	Move to a new city	Have children
Get a driver's license	Travel abroad	Retire

Which of these events are the most important changes? Why?
What changes have you gone through in the last year? Which do you expect to happen soon?
What other things bring about change in our lives?

2 CONVERSATION I haven't seen you in ages.

A Listen and practice.

Hayden: Hey, Thomas! I haven't seen you since you changed schools! How have you been?

Thomas: Not bad. How about you? Have you finished college?

Hayden: Yeah. I majored in business administration, and I've just started a new job. How about you? Are you still in college?

Thomas: Oh, no, I finished school. I majored in drama. Actually, I'm in a play right now.

Hayden: No kidding! What's the name of the play? I'd love to see it!

Thomas: I'm acting in *A Change for the Better* at the Atlas Theater.

Hayden: Cool! You know, you look different. Have you changed your hair?

Thomas: Yeah, it's longer now. My character has long hair. And I wear contacts.

Hayden: Well, you look fantastic!

Thomas: Thanks, so do you!

B Listen to the rest of the conversation. What are some other changes in Hayden's life?

3 GRAMMAR FOCUS

Describing changes

With the present tense

I**'m not** in school anymore.

I **wear** contacts now.

With the past tense

I **majored** in business administration.

I **got** engaged.

With the present perfect

I**'ve** just **started** a new job.

I**'ve bought** a new apartment.

With the comparative

It's **less noisy** than downtown.

My hair is **longer** now.

GRAMMAR PLUS *see page 147*

A How have you changed in the last five years? Check (✓) the statements that are true for you. If a statement isn't true, give the correct information.

- [ ] **1.** I dress differently now.
- [ ] **2.** I've changed my hairstyle.
- [ ] **3.** I've made some new friends.
- [ ] **4.** I got a pet.
- [ ] **5.** I've joined a gym.
- [ ] **6.** I moved into my own apartment.
- [ ] **7.** I'm more outgoing than before.
- [ ] **8.** I'm not in high school anymore.
- [ ] **9.** My life is easier now.
- [ ] **10.** I got married.

B **PAIR WORK** Compare your responses in part A. Have you changed in similar ways?

C **GROUP WORK** Write five sentences describing other changes in your life. Then compare in groups. Who in the group has changed the most?

4 LISTENING Online photo albums

Madison and Zachary are looking through online photo albums. Listen to their conversation. How have they changed? Write down three changes.

Changes

____

____

____

5 WORD POWER Changes

A Complete the word map with phrases from the list. Then add two more examples to each category.

dye my hair
get a bank loan
get a credit card
get a pay raise
grow a beard
improve my English vocabulary
learn a new sport
learn how to dance
open a savings account
pierce my ears
start a new online course
wear contact lenses

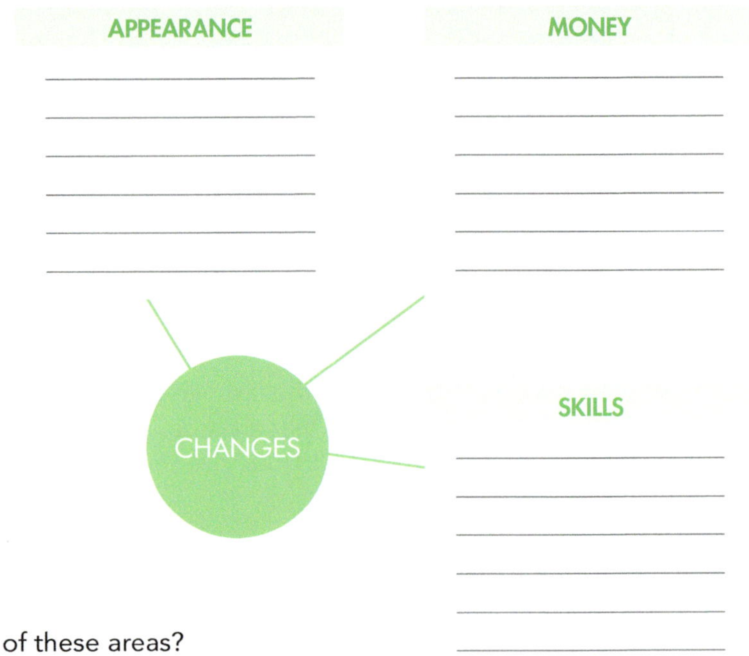

B **PAIR WORK** Have you changed in any of these areas? Tell your partner about a change in each category.

A: I started an Italian cooking class last month. I've always loved Italian food.
B: I've improved my English vocabulary a lot. I always watch movies with English subtitles now.

6 CONVERSATION Planning your future

A Listen and practice.

Matt: So, what are you going to do this year? Any New Year's resolutions?
Robin: Well, I'd love to learn how to play the guitar, so I plan to take lessons.
Matt: That sounds great. I don't have any musical talents, but I'd like to learn how to dance. Maybe I can learn to salsa!
Robin: Why not? I hope to learn to play some Latin music, too.
Matt: I know! We can take a trip to Puerto Rico and spend a month learning guitar and dancing. How about that?
Robin: Uh . . . Matt? I don't have any money. Do you?
Matt: I don't either, but I hope to get a new job soon.
Robin: Have you started looking?
Matt: Not yet, but I plan to start right after the holidays.

B Listen to the rest of the conversation. What kind of job does Matt want? What other plans does Robin have for the new year?

7 GRAMMAR FOCUS

Verb + infinitive

What **are** you **going to do** this year?

I**'m** (not) **going to take** a trip to the Caribbean.
I (don't) **plan to take** guitar lessons.
I (don't) **want to learn** to dance.

I **hope to get** a new job.
I**'d like to travel** around the United States.
I**'d love to play** the guitar.

GRAMMAR PLUS *see page 147*

A Complete these statements so that they are true for you. Use verb + infinitive as shown in the grammar box. Then add two more statements of your own.

1. I ______________ travel abroad.
2. I ______________ live with my parents.
3. I ______________ get married.
4. I ______________ have a lot of children.
5. I ______________ make a lot of money!
6. I ______________ become famous.
7. I ______________ buy a sports car.
8. I ______________ learn another language.
9. ________________________________
10. ________________________________

B **PAIR WORK** Compare your responses with a partner. How are you the same? How are you different?

C **GROUP WORK** What are your plans for the future? Take turns asking and answering these questions.

What are you going to do after this English class is over?
Do you plan to study English again next year?
What other languages would you like to learn?
What countries would you like to visit? Why?
Do you want to get a (new) job in a few years?
What other changes do you hope to make in your life? Why?

8 PRONUNCIATION Vowel sounds /oʊ/ and /ʌ/

A Many words spelled with *o* are pronounced /oʊ/ or /ʌ/. Listen to the difference and practice.

/oʊ/ = don't	smoke	go	loan	own	hope
/ʌ/ = month	love	some	does	young	touch

B Listen to these words. Check (✓) the correct pronunciation.

	both	cold	come	home	honey	money	mother	over
/oʊ/	☐	☐	☐	☐	☐	☐	☐	☐
/ʌ/	☐	☐	☐	☐	☐	☐	☐	☐

9 INTERCHANGE 16 Our possible future

Imagine you could do anything, go anywhere, and meet anybody.
Go to Interchange 16 on page 131.

10 SPEAKING An English course abroad

A GROUP WORK You want to take an English course abroad in an English-speaking country. Groups get special discounts, so your whole group has to agree on a trip. Talk about these details and take notes on your group's decisions.

1. Where you'd like to study (choose an English-speaking country and city)
2. When you'd like to travel (choose month of the year)
3. How long you want to stay there
4. Where you'd like to stay (choose one): a family home, a dorm, a hostel, an apartment, a hotel
5. Courses you plan to take (choose two): grammar, writing, pronunciation, conversation, business English
6. Tourist places you hope to see

A: Where would you like to study?
B: How about Australia?
C: Australia is great, but it's going to be too expensive. I'd love to go to London. I've never been there.
D: When do you want to go? I think May and June are the best months.

B CLASS ACTIVITY Present your ideas to the class. If the whole class agrees on one trip, you can get a bigger discount.

11 WRITING Travel plans

A GROUP WORK Work with the same group from Exercise 10. As a group, write to your teacher about your plans for the class trip abroad.

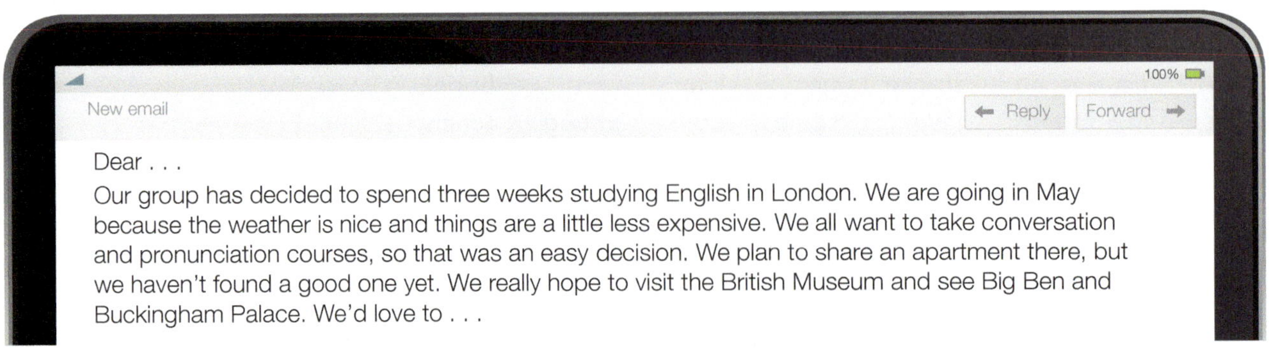

Dear . . .

Our group has decided to spend three weeks studying English in London. We are going in May because the weather is nice and things are a little less expensive. We all want to take conversation and pronunciation courses, so that was an easy decision. We plan to share an apartment there, but we haven't found a good one yet. We really hope to visit the British Museum and see Big Ben and Buckingham Palace. We'd love to . . .

B PAIR WORK Get together with a student from another group and read each other's messages. Do you have similar plans?

12 READING

A Read the article. What is it about? Check (✓) the correct answer.

☐ Students in the Netherlands ☐ An important invention ☐ Vacations near the ocean

A Goal Accomplished

Boyan Slat has one huge goal. It's a goal that could benefit people and animals all over the world. Amazingly, it looks like he's going to accomplish it.

When he was 16, Dutch engineering student Boyan Slat was on vacation in Greece, and he started to think about all the garbage that gets washed up on beaches. The oceans around the world are full of plastic – millions of tons of plastic. Unfortunately, plastic doesn't just disappear. It takes centuries to break down. Slat wanted to do something to change all that. So he made it a personal goal to clean up the garbage in the world's oceans.

Slat started with an idea for an extraordinary machine to "catch" the plastic floating in the water using the natural energy of the ocean. He left school in 2013 to begin work on his project, which he called The Ocean Cleanup.

A year later, he was leading a team of 100 scientists and engineers working on the invention. Slat needed money for this, so he started asking people to donate to his project online and raised over $2 million!

Soon after, Slat was named a "Champion of the Earth" by the United Nations. It's the most important title the UN gives to people helping the environment. The Ocean Cleanup also won several awards for having one of the best inventions of 2015. But the dream goes on for Boyan Slat. He hopes that the oceans will be free of plastic in about twenty or thirty years.

B Who do you think this article was written for? Choose (✓) the correct answer.

☐ People who care about the environment
☐ College students who want to be inventors
☐ People on vacation who hate garbage

C Read the article and answer the questions.

1. Where was Boyan Slat when he had his big idea?
2. Why did Slat leave school?
3. What is the problem with plastic?
4. How did Slat get the money for his project?
5. When does Slat hope the oceans will be clean?

D **GROUP WORK** Have you had a personal goal that you achieved? Or do you know someone who achieved an amazing personal goal? What was the goal?

Units 15–16 Progress check

SELF-ASSESSMENT

How well can you do these things? Check (✓) the boxes.

I can . . .	Very well	OK	A little
Discuss future plans and arrangements (Ex. 1)	☐	☐	☐
Make and respond to invitations (Ex. 2)	☐	☐	☐
Understand and pass on telephone messages (Ex. 3)	☐	☐	☐
Ask and answer questions about changes in my life (Ex. 4)	☐	☐	☐
Describe personal goals (Ex. 5)	☐	☐	☐
Discuss and decide how to accomplish goals (Ex. 5)	☐	☐	☐

1 DISCUSSION The weekend

A GROUP WORK Find out what your classmates are doing this weekend. Ask for details about each person's plans.

Name	Plans	Details

A: What are you going to do this weekend?
B: I'm watching a soccer game on Sunday.
C: Who's playing?

B GROUP WORK Whose weekend plans sound the best? Why?

2 ROLE PLAY Inviting a friend

Student A: Invite Student B to one of the events from Exercise 1. Say where and when it is.

Student B: Student A invites you out. Accept and ask for more information, or refuse and give an excuse.

Change roles and try the role play again.

3 LISTENING Matthew isn't here.

Listen to the phone conversations. Write down the messages.

1

Message for: ____________________
Caller: ____________________
Message: ____________________
____
____

2

Message for: ____________________
Caller: ____________________
Message: ____________________
____
____

4 SURVEY Changes

A **CLASS ACTIVITY** Go around the class and find this information. Write a classmate's name only once. Ask follow-up questions.

Find someone who . . .	Name
1. doesn't wear glasses anymore	
2. goes out more often these days	
3. got his or her hair cut last month	
4. got married last year	
5. has changed schools recently	
6. has gotten a part-time job recently	
7. has started a new hobby	
8. is happier these days	

B **CLASS ACTIVITY** Compare your information. Who in the class has changed the most?

5 SPEAKING Setting goals

Check (✓) the goals you have and add two more. Then choose one goal. Plan how to accomplish it with a partner.

- ☐ get into a good school
- ☐ have more free time
- ☐ have more friends
- ☐ move to a new city
- ☐ own my own apartment
- ☐ travel a lot more
- ☐ live a long time
- ☐ ____________________
- ☐ ____________________

A: I'd like to have more free time.
B: How are you going to do that?

WHAT'S NEXT?

Look at your Self-assessment again. Do you need to review anything?

Interchange activities

INTERCHANGE 1 Getting to know you

A **CLASS ACTIVITY** Add one more question to the chart. Go around the class and interview three classmates. Complete the chart.

	Classmate 1	Classmate 2	Classmate 3
What's your first name?			
What's your last name?			
What city are you from?			
When's your birthday?			
What's your favorite color?			
What are your hobbies?			
________________			

B **GROUP WORK** Compare your information. Then discuss these questions.

Who . . . ?

has a long first name
has a long last name
is not from a big city
has the next birthday
likes orange or brown
has an interesting hobby

INTERCHANGE 2 What we have in common

A CLASS ACTIVITY Add one more question to the chart. Answer these questions about yourself. Then interview two classmates. Write their names and the times they do each thing.

What time do you . . . ?	Me	Name ________	Name ________
get up during the week			
get up on weekends			
have breakfast			
leave for school or work			
get home during the week			
have dinner			
go to bed during the week			
________________			

B PAIR WORK Whose schedule is similar to yours? Tell your partner.

A: Amir and I have similar schedules. We both get up at 7:00 and have breakfast at 7:30.

B: I leave for work at 7:30, but Nikki leaves for school at . . .

useful expressions

We both . . . at . . .

We . . . at different times.

My schedule is different from my two classmates' schedules.

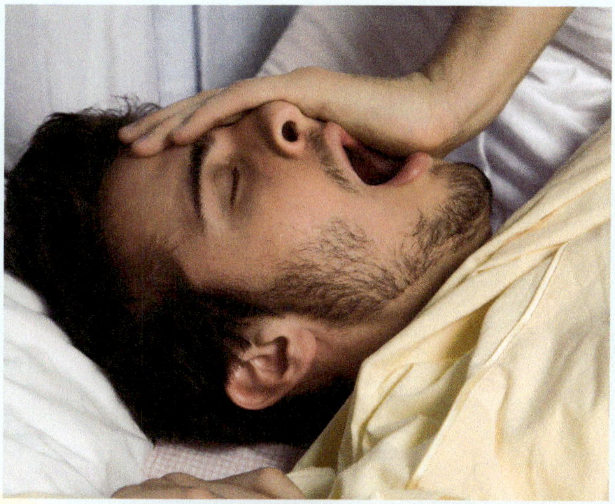

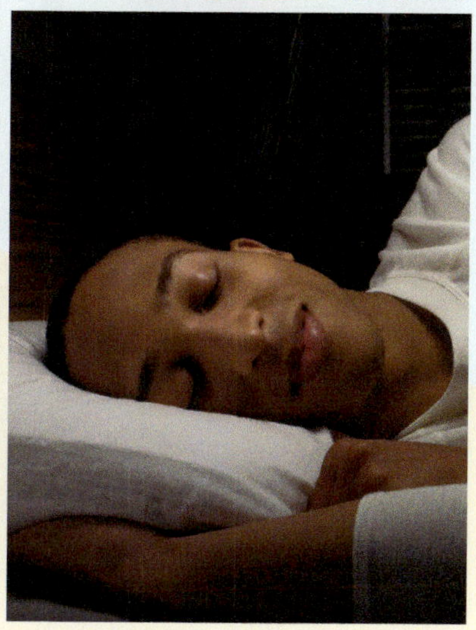

INTERCHANGE 3 Flea market

STUDENT A

A You want to sell these things. Write your "asking price" for each item.

TABLET
asking price: ______
sold for: ______

HEADPHONES
asking price: ______
sold for: ______

ARMCHAIR
asking price: ______
sold for: ______

SKATEBOARD
asking price: ______
sold for: ______

STUDENT B

A You want to sell these things. Write your "asking price" for each item.

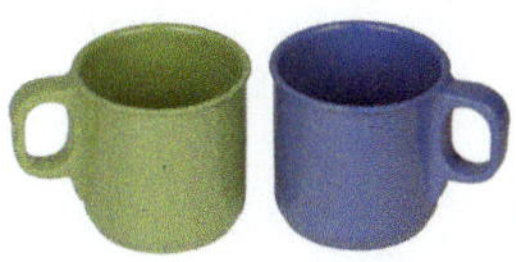

MUGS
asking price: ______
sold for: ______

PRINTER
asking price: ______
sold for: ______

ELECTRIC GUITAR
asking price: ______
sold for: ______

TREADMILL
asking price: ______
sold for: ______

STUDENTS A AND B

B **PAIR WORK** Now choose three things you want to buy. Get the best price for each one. Then write what each item "sold for" on the price tag.

A: How much is the tablet computer?
B: It's only $70.
A: Wow! That's expensive!
B: Well, how about $35?
A: No. That's still too much. I'll give you $30 for it.
B: Sold! It's yours.

C **GROUP WORK** Compare your earnings in groups. Who made the most money at the flea market?

INTERCHANGE 4 Are you free this weekend?

go bike riding

go to a street fair

go dancing

do the laundry

clean the house

A Write three things you need to do and three things you want to do this weekend. Include the days of the week and the times.

I need to . . .	I want to . . .

B **PAIR WORK** Invite your partner to do things on the weekend. Accept or decline invitations. If you decline an invitation, explain why. Agree on two activities to do together.

A: Would you like to see a movie on Saturday at 8:00 P.M.?

B: I'd like to, but I need to study for a test. Would you like to go to the park on Sunday at 10:00 A.M.?

A: Yes, I would. And would you like to . . . ?

C **GROUP WORK** Get together with another pair. Can you agree on two things to do together?

D **CLASS WORK** Explain your group's choices to the class.
"Eu-jin wanted to go to the park on Sunday at 10 A.M., but Serhat needs to visit his aunt on Sunday morning, so we're going out for lunch on Sunday at . . ."

INTERCHANGE 5 Is that true?

CLASS ACTIVITY Go around the class telling your classmates three activities that members of your family are doing these days. Two activities have to be true, but one needs to be false! Can your classmates guess which activity is false with only two questions?

learning a foreign language

raising a child

renovating the house

working in another country

writing a blog

your ideas

learning to drive

going to college

traveling around the world

playing in a band

playing on a team

A: My brother is working in Berlin and his wife is studying German there. My niece is learning three languages at school: German, English, and Spanish.

B: Is your brother really working in Berlin?

A: Yes, he is.

B: Is your niece really learning Spanish?

A: No, she's not! She's learning German and English, but she isn't learning Spanish.

INTERCHANGE 6 What's your talent?

A **CLASS ACTIVITY** Add two items to the chart. Does anyone in your class do these things? How often and how well? Go around the class and find one person for each activity.

	Name	How often?	How well?
bake cookies			
cook			
cut hair			
do card tricks			
fix things			
play an instrument			
sing			
do yoga			

A: Do you bake cookies?
B: Yes, I do.
A: How often do you bake cookies?
B: Once a month.
A: Really? And how well do you bake?

B **GROUP WORK** Imagine there's a fundraiser to buy new books for the school library this weekend. Who do you think can help? Choose three people from your class. Explain your choices.

A: Let's ask Lydia to help with the fundraiser.
B: Why Lydia?
A: Because she bakes cookies very well.
C: Yes, she really does. And Mariana is very good at fixing things. Let's ask her, too!

INTERCHANGE 7 Memories

GROUP WORK Play the board game. Follow these instructions.

1. Write your initials on small pieces of paper. These are your game pieces.
2. Take turns by tossing a coin: If the coin lands face up, move two spaces. If the coin lands face down, move one space.
3. When you land on a space, answer the question. Answer any follow-up questions.
4. If you land on "Free question," another player asks you any question.

A: I'll go first. OK, one space. Last night, I met my best friend.
B: Oh, yeah? Where did you go?
A: We went to the movies.

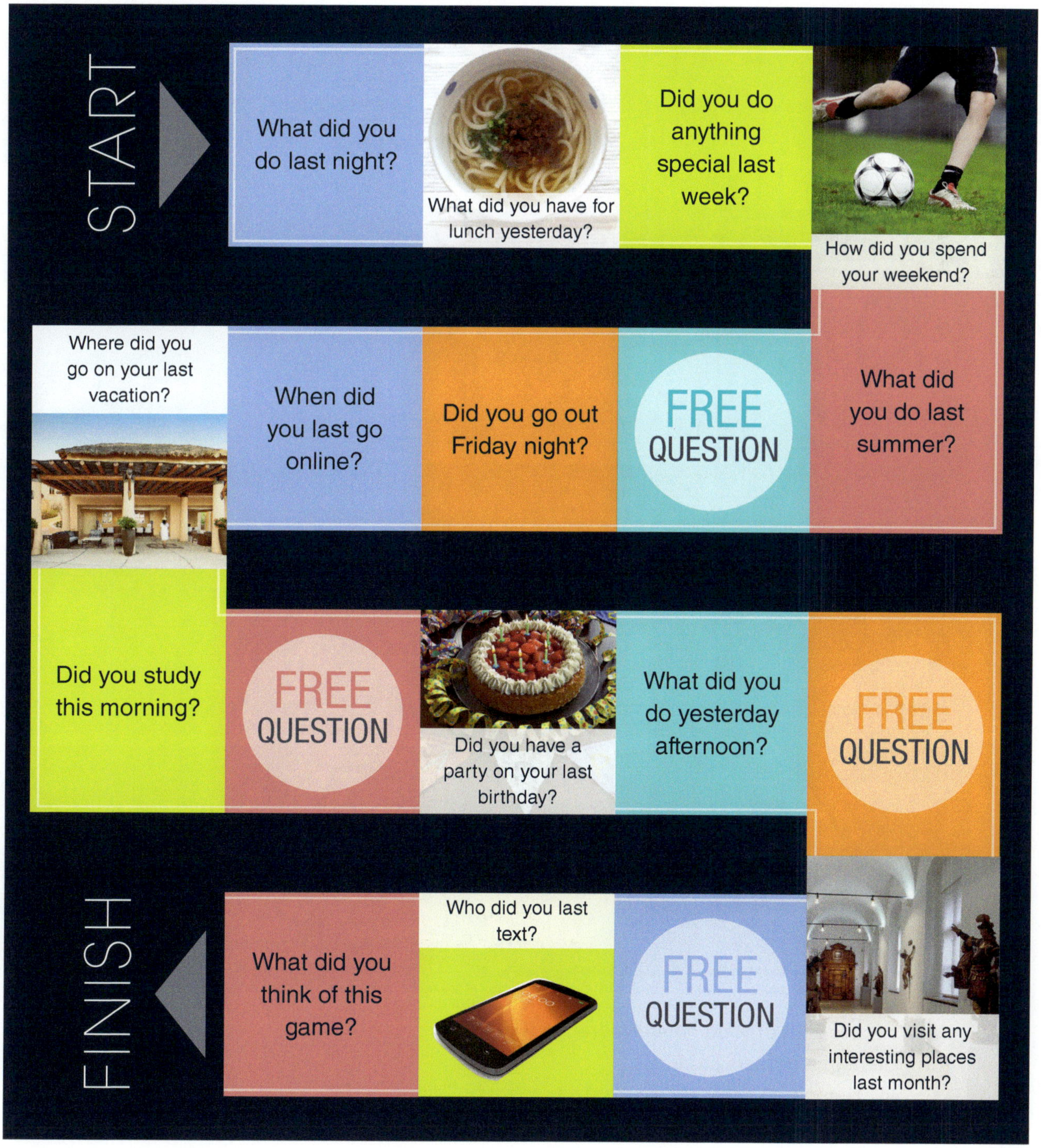

INTERCHANGE 8 Where are we?

CLASS ACTIVITY Play a guessing game. Follow these instructions.

1. Get into two teams, A and B.
2. Each team chooses one of the locations below. Keep it a secret!
3. Each team chooses a teammate to guess the other team's location. He or she is the guesser.
4. Show your location to all the students on the other team, except their guesser.
5. Take turns giving your guessers one clue at a time until they guess the location. Use *There is/ There are* plus a quantifier. You cannot give more than 10 clues. Your team can get 1 to 10 points, depending on how many clues you need to give your guesser (1 clue = 1 point) before he or she guesses the right location. Remember: you don't want to get many points!
6. At the end of the game, the team with fewer points wins.

an airport

a bank

a bookstore

a café

a clothing store

a drugstore

a grocery store

a gym

a hair salon

a hospital

a movie theater

a newstand

an outdoor market

a park

a shopping mall

a stadium

A: There is a lot of food here. Where are we?
B: You're in a grocery store.
C: No. There aren't any walls here. This isn't a building.
B: You're at an outdoor market!
A: Correct! We're at an outdoor market.

INTERCHANGE 9A Find the differences

STUDENT A

A PAIR WORK How many differences can you find between your picture here and your partner's picture? Ask questions like these to find the differences.

How many people are standing / sitting / wearing . . . / holding a drink? Who?
What color is . . . 's T-shirt / sweater / hair?
Does . . . wear glasses / have a beard / have long hair?
What does . . . look like?

B CLASS ACTIVITY How many differences are there in the pictures?
"In picture 1, Daniel's T-shirt is . . . In picture 2, it's . . ."

INTERCHANGE 9B Find the differences

STUDENT B

A **PAIR WORK** How many differences can you find between your picture here and your partner's picture? Ask questions like these to find the differences.

How many people are standing / sitting / wearing . . . / holding a drink? Who?
What color is . . .'s T-shirt / sweater / hair?
Does . . . wear glasses / have a beard / have long hair?
What does . . . look like?

B **CLASS ACTIVITY** How many differences are there in the pictures?
"In picture 1, Daniel's shirt is . . . In picture 2, it's . . ."

INTERCHANGE 10 Fun survey

A **PAIR WORK** How much fun does your partner have? Interview him or her. Write the number of points using this scale.

never = 1 point	4–7 times = 3 points
1–3 times = 2 points	8 or more times = 4 points

Home Posts News Contact us Log in

SURVEY

HOW MANY TIMES HAVE YOU . . .	POINTS
1. watched a really good movie or TV show in the last two months?	______
2. listened to your favorite kind of music in the last week?	______
3. talked to your best friend in the last two weeks?	______
4. read something interesting that wasn't for work or school in the last month?	______
5. eaten your favorite foods in the last three weeks?	______
6. had a really fun weekend in the last three months?	______
7. spent at least one hour doing something you like in the last three days?	______
8. taken a relaxing vacation in the last year?	______
9. had a good laugh in the last 24 hours?	______
10. told yourself "This is fun!" in the last 12 hours?	______

B **GROUP WORK** Add up your partner's points. Tell the group how much fun your partner has and why.

10–19 = You don't have enough fun. You should try to do things you enjoy more often! Stop and smell the roses!

20–29 = You have fun sometimes, but you need to do it more often. Continue to take time to do the things that you like.

30–40 = You know how to have fun! You know how to have a good time and enjoy life. Keep it up!

"Ellen has fun sometimes. She watches her favorite TV show once a week and takes a vacation twice a year. But she never reads anything she really likes – only the things she has to read for school."

C **CLASS ACTIVITY** Do you think your partner needs to have more fun? In what way?

"I think Ellen needs to have more fun in her life. She needs to spend more time doing things she likes. And she needs to eat her favorite foods more often. She also . . ."

INTERCHANGE 11 Welcome to our city!

A **PAIR WORK** You want to attract more visitors to your city or town. Complete the sentences below and add one more sentence to write a guide for tourists.

WELCOME TO OUR CITY!

LOGIN / REGISTER

It's a really ____________ place and you will find ____________ to do here.

The weather is ____________ and the best times of the year to visit are ____________ and ____________.

You can ____________, ____________, and ____________, and you shouldn't miss the famous ____________!

Don't forget to try our local food! ____________ can be a little expensive, though, but you can have a good meal for a reasonable price at ____________.

Also, ______________________________.

Enjoy your stay and come back soon!

B **CLASS ACTIVITY** Read your guide to the class. Ask follow-up questions to learn more.

What is the first place you should visit?
What is an exciting place to have fun on a Saturday night?
What is a relaxing place to visit on a Sunday morning?
What is a quiet place to study or do some work?
What is a really beautiful area that you shouldn't miss?
What is a dangerous area that you should avoid?
What places are usually too crowded?
Where can you exercise outdoors?
What fun things can you do for free?
Where's a popular place to meet?

C **CLASS ACTIVITY** Which are your two favorite guides? Which details did you find especially interesting about them?

INTERCHANGE 12 What should I do?

A GROUP WORK Play the board game. Follow these instructions.

1. Write your initials on small pieces of paper. These are your game pieces.
2. Take turns by tossing a coin: If the coin lands face up, move two spaces. If the coin lands face down, move one space.
3. When you land on a space, ask two others in your group for advice.
4. The first person to cross the finish line is the winner.

A: I have the hiccups, Hiroto. What should I do?
B: Well, it's sometimes useful to hold your breath.
A: Thanks. What about you, Erica? What's your advice?
C: You should drink some water. That always works for me.

useful expressions

You should . . .
You could . . .
It's a good idea to . . .
It's important to . . .
I think it's useful to . . .

B CLASS ACTIVITY Who gave the best advice in your group? Tell the class.

INTERCHANGE 13 Planning a food festival

A PAIR WORK Imagine your class is organizing a food festival with different food trucks. You and your classmate are responsible for one of the trucks. Choose a name for your truck. Write it at the top of the menu. Then, write the food and drinks you'd like to sell at your truck. Then write the prices.

B GROUP WORK Trade your menus with another pair. Order food and drinks from their menu, and then leave some suggestions about the menu on the message board.

____

(write the name of your food truck here)

FOOD	PRICE

DRINKS	PRICE

CUSTOMERS' SUGGESTIONS

INTERCHANGE 14 How much do you know?

A PAIR WORK Take turns asking and answering these questions. Check (✓) the answer you think is correct for each question. Then write two more questions and answers.

World Knowledge Quiz

1.	Which place is the wettest?	☐ Kaua'i, Hawai'i	☐ Manaus, Brazil	☐ Emei Shan, China
2.	Which country is the hottest?	☐ Algeria	☐ Libya	☐ Somalia
3.	Which country is closest to the equator?	☐ Colombia	☐ India	☐ Malaysia
4.	Which animal is the biggest?	☐ a bison	☐ an elephant	☐ a blue whale
5.	Which animal lives the longest?	☐ an elephant	☐ a tortoise	☐ a green iguana
6.	Which mountain range is the longest?	☐ the Andes	☐ the Himalayas	☐ the Rockies
7.	Which planet is the smallest?	☐ Earth	☐ Mercury	☐ Venus
8.	Which planet is the largest?	☐ Jupiter	☐ Neptune	☐ Saturn
9.	Which city is the oldest?	☐ Beijing, China	☐ Luxor, Egypt	☐ Rome, Italy
10.	Which metal is the heaviest?	☐ aluminum	☐ gold	☐ silver
11.	______________	________	________	________
12.	______________	________	________	________

1. Kaua'i, Hawai'i
2. Lybia
3. Colombia
4. a blue whale
5. a tortoise
6. the Andes
7. Mercury
8. Jupiter
9. Luxor, Egypt
10. gold

B PAIR WORK Check your answers. You and your partner get a point for every correct answer.

C CLASS ACTIVITY Ask your classmates your two questions. Get a point for every question nobody can answer correctly.

INTERCHANGE 15 Weekend plans

CLASS ACTIVITY What are your classmates' plans for the weekend? Add two activities to the list. Then go around the class and find people who are going to do these things. For each question, ask for more information and take notes.

Find someone who's going to . . .	Name	Notes
go to a party		
go out of town		
go shopping		
see a live performance		
see/watch a movie		
see/watch a game		
meet friends		
visit relatives		
clean the house		
study for a test		

A: Samira, are you going to a party this weekend?
B: Yes, I am.
A: Where is the party going to be?
B: At my friend Lila's place. She's having a party to celebrate her birthday.

INTERCHANGE 16 Our possible future

A PAIR WORK Talk with your partner and complete this chart with two ideas for each question – your idea and your partner's idea.

What is . . .	You	Your partner
something you plan to do next year?		
something you aren't going to do next year?		
something you hope to buy in the next year?		
something you would like to change about yourself?		
something you would like to learn?		
a place you would like to visit someday?		
a city you would like to live in someday?		
a job you would like to have?		
a goal you hope to achieve?		

A: What is something you plan to do next year?
B: Well, I'm going to travel to Morocco.
A: Oh, really? Where in Morocco?
B: I'm not sure yet! What about you? What do you plan to do next year?
A: I'd like to get my own place.
B: Oh, really? Are you planning to rent an apartment?
A: No, actually I'm going to buy one.
B: Good for you!

B GROUP ACTIVITY Compare your information with another pair. Explain your goals and plans.

A: What are two things you plan to do next year?
B: Well, I'm going to visit Morocco, and Helena is going to get her own place.
C: That's right. I'm going to buy a small apartment. And you?
A: Well, I . . .

Grammar plus

UNIT 1

1 Statements with *be*; possessive adjectives page 3

- Don't confuse contractions of *be* with possessive adjectives: **You're** a student. **Your** class is English 1. (NOT: ~~You're class is English 1.~~) **He's** my classmate. **His** name is Ricardo. (NOT: ~~He's name is Ricardo.~~)

Choose the correct words.

1. This (**is**) / **are** Dulce Castelo. **She's** / **Her** a new student from Santo Domingo.
2. My name **am** / **is** Sergio. **I'm** / **He's** from Brazil.
3. My brother and I **is** / **are** students here. **Our** / **We're** names are Nate and Chad.
4. **He's** / **His** Kento. **He's** / **His** 19 years old.
5. **They're** / **Their** in my English class. **It's** / **Its** a big class.

2 Wh-questions with *be* page 4

- Use *What* to ask about things: **What's** in your bag? Use *Where* to ask about places: **Where's** your friend from? Use *Who* to ask about people: **Who's** your teacher? Use *What . . . like?* to ask for a description: **What's** your friend **like**?

Match the questions with the answers.

1. Who's that? ___f___
2. Where's your teacher? _______
3. What are your friends like? _______
4. Where's she from? _______
5. Who are they? _______
6. What's his name? _______

a. They're really nice.
b. She's from South Korea.
c. They're my brother and sister.
d. His name is Daniel.
e. He's in class.
f. That's our new classmate.

3 Yes/No questions and short answers with *be* page 5

- Use short answers to answer yes/no questions. Don't use contractions with short answers with Yes: **Are you** from Mexico? Yes, **I am**. (NOT: ~~Yes, I'm.~~)

Complete the conversations.

1. **A:** ___Are they___ in your class?
   B: No, _____________. They're in English 2.
2. **A:** Hi! _____________ in this class?
   B: Yes, _____________. I'm a new student here.
3. **A:** _____________ from the United States?
   B: No, _____________. We're from Calgary, Canada.
4. **A:** Hi, Monica. _____________ free?
   B: No, _____________. I'm on my way to class.
5. **A:** That's the new student. _____________ from Paraguay?
   B: No, _____________. He's from Uruguay.
6. **A:** _____________ from Indonesia?
   B: Yes, _____________. She's from Jakarta.

UNIT 2

1 Simple present Wh-questions and statements page 10

Statements

- Verbs with *he/she/it* end in *–s*: He/She **walks** to school. BUT I/You/We/They **walk** to school.
- *Have*, *go*, and *do* are irregular with *he/she/it*: She **has** a class at 1:00. He **goes** to school at night. She **does** her homework before school.

Wh-questions

- Use *does* in questions with *he/she/it* and *do* with all the others: Where does he/she/it live? Where do I/you/we/they live?
- Don't add *–s* to the verb: Where does she **live**? (NOT: ~~Where does she lives~~?)

Complete the conversations with the correct form of the verbs in parentheses.

1. A: I ___*have*___ (have) good news! Mona ______ (have) a new job.
   B: How ______ she ______ (like) it?
   A: She ______ (love) it. The hours are great.
   B: What time ______ she ______ (start)?
   A: She ______ (start) at ten and ______ (finish) at four.
2. A: What ______ you ______ (do)?
   B: I'm a teacher.
   A: What ______ you ______ (teach)?
   B: I ______ (teach) Spanish and English.
   A: Really? My sister ______ (teach) English, too.

2 Time expressions page 12

- Use *in* with *the morning/afternoon/evening*. Use *at* with *night*: He goes to school **in** the afternoon and works **at** night. BUT: **on** Friday night.
- Use *at* with clock times: She gets up **at** 7:00.
- Use *on* with days: He gets up early **on** weekdays. She has class **on** Mondays.

Complete the conversation with time expressions from the box.
You can use some words more than once.

at early in on until

A: How's your new job?
B: I love it, but the hours are difficult. I start work ______ 6:30 A.M., and I work ______ 3:30.
A: That's interesting! I work the same hours, but I work ______ night. I start ______ 6:30 ______ the evening and finish ______ 3:30 ______ the morning.
B: Wow! What time do you get up?
A: Well, I get home ______ 4:30 and go to bed ______ 5:30. And I sleep ______ 2:00. But I only work ______ weekends, so it's OK. What about you?
B: Oh, I work ______ Monday, Wednesday, and Friday. And I get up ______ – around 5:00 A.M.

UNIT 3

1 Demonstratives; *one, ones* page 17

- With singular nouns, use *this* for a thing that is nearby and *that* for a thing that is not nearby: How much is **this** hat here? How much is **that** hat over there?
- With plural nouns, use *these* for things that are nearby and *those* for things that are not nearby: How much are **these** earrings here? How much are **those** earrings over there?
- Use *one* to replace a singular noun: I like the red hat. I like the red **one**. Use *ones* to replace plural nouns: I like the green bags. I like the green **ones**.

Choose the correct words.

1. **A:** Excuse me. How much are **this** / **these** shoes?
   B: **It's** / **They're** $279.
   A: And how much is **this** / **that** bag over there?
   B: **It's** / **They're** only $129.
   A: And are the two gray **one** / **ones** $129, too?
   B: No. **That** / **Those** are only $119.
   A: Oh! **This** / **That** store is really expensive.
2. **A:** Can I help you?
   B: Yes, please. I really like **these** / **those** jeans over there. How much **is it** / **are they**?
   A: Which **one** / **ones**? Do you mean **this** / **these**?
   B: No, the black **one** / **ones**.
   A: Let me look. Oh, **it's** / **they're** $35.99.
   B: That's not bad. And how much is **this** / **that** sweater here?
   A: **It's** / **They're** only $9.99.

2 Preferences; comparisons with adjectives page 20

- For adjectives with one syllable or adjectives of two syllables ending in *–y*, add *–er* to form the comparative:
  cheap → cheaper; nice → nicer; big → bigger, pretty → prettier.
- For adjectives with two syllables not ending in *–y* or adjectives of three or more syllables, use *more* + adjective to form the comparative: stylish → more stylish, expensive → more expensive.

A Write the comparatives of these adjectives.

1. attractive ___more attractive___
2. happy ____________
3. exciting ____________
4. friendly ____________
5. interesting ____________
6. reasonable ____________
7. sad ____________
8. warm ____________

B Answer the questions. Use the first word in the parentheses in your answer. Then write another sentence with the second word.

1. Which pants do you prefer, the cotton ones or the wool ones? (wool / attractive)
   I prefer the wool ones. They're more attractive than the cotton ones.
2. Which ring do you like better, the gold one or the silver one? (silver / interesting)
   ____
3. Which one do you prefer, the silk blouse or the cotton blouse? (silk / pretty)
   ____
4. Which ones do you like more, the black shoes or the purple ones? (purple / cheap)
   ____

UNIT 4

1 Simple present questions; short answers page 23

- Use *do* + base form for yes/no questions and short answers with *I/you/we/they*: **Do** I/you/we/they **like** rock? Yes, I/you/we/they **do**. No, I/you/we/they **don't.**
- Use *does* in yes/no questions and short answers with *he/she/it*: **Does** he/she **like** rock? Yes, he/she **does**. No, he/she **doesn't.**
- Use *don't* and *doesn't* + base form for negative statements: I **don't** like horror movies. He **doesn't like** action movies.
- Remember: Don't add *–s* to the base form: Does she **like** rock? (NOT: ~~Does she likes rock~~?)
- Subject pronouns (*I, you, he, she, it, we, they*) usually come before a verb. Object pronouns (*me, you, him, her, it, us, them*) usually come after a verb: He likes **her**, but she doesn't like **him**.

A Complete the questions and short answers.

1. **A:** Do you play (play) a musical instrument?
   B: Yes, I do. I play the guitar.
2. **A:** ______________ (like) Carrie Underwood?
   B: No, ______________. John doesn't like country music.
3. **A:** ______________ (like) talk shows?
   B: Yes, ______________. Lisa is a big fan of them.
4. **A:** ______________ (watch) the news on TV?
   B: Yes, ______________. Kevin and I watch the news every night.
5. **A:** ______________ (like) hip-hop?
   B: No, ______________. But I love R&B.
6. **A:** ______________ (listen to) jazz?
   B: No, ______________. But my parents listen to a lot of classical music.

B Complete the sentences with object pronouns.

1. We don't listen to hip-hop because we really don't like it.
2. We love your voice. Please sing for ________.
3. These sunglasses are great. Do you like ________?
4. Who is that man? Do you know ________?
5. Beth looks great in green. It's a really good color for ________.

2 *Would*; verb + *to* + verb page 26

- Don't use a contraction in affirmative short answers with *would*: **Would** you **like to go to** the game? Yes, I **would**. (NOT: ~~Yes, I'd~~.)

Unscramble the questions and answers to complete the conversation.

A: tonight to see would you like with me a movie
____?

B: I would. yes, what to see would you like
____?

A: the new Matt Damon movie to see I'd like
____.

B: OK. That's a great idea!

UNIT 5

1 Present continuous page 32

- Use the present continuous to talk about actions that are happening now: What **are** you **doing (these days)**? **I'm studying** English.
- The present continuous is present of *be* + *–ing*. For verbs ending in *e*, drop the *e* and add *–ing*: have ⟶ having, live ⟶ living.
- For verbs ending in vowel + consonant, double the consonant and add *–ing*: sit ⟶ sitting.

Write questions with the words in parentheses and the present continuous. Then complete the responses with short answers or the verbs in the box.

live study take ✓ teach work

1. **A:** (what / your sister / do / these days) What's your sister doing these days?
   B: She's teaching English.
   A: Really? (she / live / abroad) ______
   B: Yes, ______. She ______ in South Korea.
2. **A:** (how / you / spend / your summer) ______
   B: I ______ part-time. I ______ two classes also.
   A: (what / you / take) ______
   B: My friend and I ______ photography and Japanese. We like our classes a lot.

2 Quantifiers page 34

- Use *a lot of, all, few, nearly all* before plural nouns: **A lot of/All/Few/Nearly all** families are small. Use *no one* before a verb: **No one** gets married before the age of 18.
- *Nearly all* means "almost all."

Read the sentences about the small town of Monroe. Rewrite the sentences using the quantifiers in the box. Use each quantifier only once.

a lot of all few nearly all ✓ no one

1. In Monroe, 0% of the people drive before the age of 16.
   In Monroe, no one drives before the age of 16.
2. Ninety-eight percent of students finish high school.
   ______
3. One hundred percent of children start school by the age of six.
   ______
4. Eighty-nine percent of couples have more than one child.
   ______
5. Five percent of families have more than four children.
   ______

UNIT 6

1 Adverbs of frequency page 37

- Adverbs of frequency (*always, almost always, usually, often, sometimes, hardly ever, almost never, never*) usually come before the main verb: She **never plays** tennis. I **almost always eat** breakfast. BUT Adverbs of frequency usually come after the verb *be*: I**'m always** late.
- *Usually* and *sometimes* can begin a sentence: **Usually** I walk to work. **Sometimes** I exercise in the morning.
- Some frequency expressions usually come at the end of a sentence: *every day, once a week, twice a month, three times a year:* Do you exercise **every day**? I exercise **three times a week**.

Put the words in order to make questions. Then complete the answers with the words in parentheses.

1. you what weekends usually do do on
   Q: *What do you usually do on weekends?*
   A: I ____________________ (often / play sports)
2. ever you go jogging do with a friend
   Q: ____________________
   A: No, ____________________ (always / alone)
3. you play do basketball how often
   Q: ____________________
   A: I ____________________ (four times a week)
4. do you what in the evening usually do
   Q: ____________________
   A: My family and I ____________________ (almost always / go online)
5. go how often you do to the gym
   Q: ____________________
   A: I ____________________ (never)

2 Questions with *how*; short answers page 40

- Don't confuse *good* and *well*. Use the adjective *good* with *be* and the adverb *well* with other verbs: How **good** are you at soccer? BUT How **well** do you play soccer?

Complete the questions with *How* and a word from the box. Then match the questions and the answers.

good long often well

1. __________ do you lift weights? _____
2. __________ do you play basketball? _____
3. __________ are you at volleyball? _____
4. __________ do you spend at the gym? _____

a. Not very well, but I love it.
b. About six hours a week.
c. Not very often. I prefer martial arts.
d. Pretty good, but I hate it.

UNIT 7

1 Simple past page 45

- Use *did* with the base form – not the past form – of the main verb in questions: How **did** you **spend** the weekend? (NOT: ~~How did you spent~~ . . .?)
- Use *didn't* with the base form in negative statements: We **didn't go** shopping. (NOT: ~~We didn't went shopping~~.)

Complete the conversation.

A: ___Did___ you ___have___ (have) a good weekend?
B: Yes, I ________ . I ________ (have) a great time. My sister and I ________ (go) shopping on Saturday. We ________ (spend) all day at the mall.
A: ________ you ________ (buy) anything special?
B: I ________ (buy) a new laptop. And I ________ (get) some new clothes, too.
A: Lucky you! What clothes ________ you ________ (buy)?
B: Well, I ________ (need) some new boots. I ________ (get) some great ones at Great Times Department Store. What about you? What ________ you ________ (do) on Saturday?
A: I ________ (not, do) anything special. I ________ (stay) home and ________ (work) around the house. Oh, but I ________ (see) a really good movie on TV. And then I ________ (make) dinner with my mother. I actually ________ (enjoy) the day.

2 Past of *be* page 47

Present		Past
am/is	→	**was**
are	→	**were**

Rewrite the sentences. Find another way to write each sentence using *was, wasn't, were,* or *weren't* and the words in parentheses.

1. Bruno didn't come to class yesterday. (in class)
   Bruno wasn't in class yesterday.
2. He worked all day. (at work)
   ____
3. Bruno and his co-workers worked on Saturday, too. (at work)
   ____
4. They didn't go to work on Sunday. (at work)
   ____
5. Did Bruno stay home on Sunday? (at home)
   ____
6. Where did Bruno go on Sunday? (on Sunday)
   ____
7. He and his brother went to a baseball game. (at a baseball game)
   ____
8. They stayed at the park until 7:00. (at the park)
   ____

UNIT 8

1 *There is, there are; one, any, some* page 51

- Don't use a contraction in a short answer with *Yes*: Is there a hotel near here? Yes, **there is**. (NOT: ~~Yes, there's~~.)
- Use *some* in affirmative statements and *any* in negative statements: There are **some** grocery stores in my neighborhood, but there aren't **any** restaurants. Use *any* in most questions: Are there **any** nice stores around here?

Complete the conversations. Choose the correct words.

1. **A:** **Is** / **Are** there any supermarkets in this neighborhood?
   B: No, there **isn't** / **aren't**, but there are **one** / **some** on Main Street.
   A: And **is** / **are** there a post office near here?
   B: Yes, **there's** / **there is**. It's across from the bank.
2. **A:** **Is** / **Are** there a gas station around here?
   B: Yes, **there's** / **there are** one behind the shopping center.
   A: Great! And are there **a** / **any** coffee shops nearby?
   B: Yes, there's a good **one** / **some** in the shopping center.

2 Quantifiers; *how many* and *how much* page 54

- Use *a lot* with both count and noncount nouns: Are there many traffic lights on First Avenue? Yes, there are **a lot**. Is there much traffic? Yes, there's **a lot**.
- Use *any* – not *none* – in negative statements: How much traffic is there on your street? There **isn't any**. = There**'s none**. (NOT: ~~There isn't none~~.)
- Use *How many* with count nouns: **How many books** do you have?
- Use *How much* with noncount nouns: **How much traffic** is there?

A Complete the conversations. Choose the correct words.

1. **A:** Is there **many** / **much** traffic in your city?
   B: Well, there's **a few** / **a little**.
2. **A:** Are there **many** / **much** Wi-Fi hotspots around here?
   B: No, there aren't **many** / **none**.
3. **A:** **How many** / **How much** restaurants are there in your neighborhood?
   B: There **is** / **are** a lot.
4. **A:** **How many** / **How much** noise **is** / **are** there in your city?
   B: There's **much** / **none**. It's very quiet.

B Write questions with the words in parentheses. Use *much* or *many*.

1. **A:** Is there much pollution in your neighborhood? (pollution)
   B: No, there isn't. My neighborhood is very clean.
2. **A:** ______________________________ (parks)
   B: Yes, there are. They're great for families.
3. **A:** ______________________________ (crime)
   B: There's none. It's a very safe part of the city.
4. **A:** ______________________________ (laundromats)
   B: There aren't any. A lot of people have their own washing machines.

UNIT 9

1 Describing people page 59

- Use *have* or *is* to describe eye and hair color: I **have** brown hair. = My hair **is** brown. He **has** blue eyes. = His eyes **are** blue.
- Don't confuse *How* and *What* in questions: **How** tall are you? (NOT: ~~What tall are you?~~) **What** color is your hair? (NOT: ~~How color is your hair?~~)

Unscramble the questions. Then write answers using the phrases in the box.

blond	brown eyes	contact lenses
✓ tall and good-looking	6 foot 2	26 – two years older than me

A: brother like look what your does
What does your brother look like?
B: *He's tall and good-looking.*
A: tall is how he
____
B: ______________________________
A: he does glasses wear
____
B: ______________________________
A: what hair color his is
____
B: ______________________________
A: he does blue have eyes
____
B: ______________________________
A: old he how is
____
B: ______________________________

2 Modifiers with participles and prepositions page 62

- Don't use a form of *be* in modifiers with participles: Sylvia is the woman **standing** near the window. (NOT: ~~Sylvia is the woman is standing near the window.~~)

Rewrite the conversations. Use the words in parentheses and *one* or *ones*.

1. **A:** Who's Carla? — **A:** *Which one is Carla?* (which)
   B: She's the woman in the red dress. — **B:** ______________ (wearing)
2. **A:** Who are your neighbors? — **A:** ______________ (which)
   B: They're the people with the baby. — **B:** ______________ (walking)
3. **A:** Who's Jeff? — **A:** ______________ (which)
   B: He's the man wearing glasses. — **B:** ______________ (with)

UNIT 10

1 Present perfect; *already, yet* page 65

- Use the present perfect for actions that happened some time in the past.
- Use *yet* in questions and negative statements: Have you checked your email **yet**? No, I haven't turned on my computer **yet**. Use *already* in affirmative statements: I've **already** checked my email.

A Complete the conversations with the present perfect of the verbs in parentheses and short answers.

1. **A:** ___Has___ Leslie ___called___ (call) you lately?
   B: No, she __________ (not call) me, but I __________ (get) some emails from her.
2. **A:** __________ you and Jan __________ (have) lunch yet?
   B: No, we __________. We're thinking of going to Tony's. __________ you __________ (try) it yet? Come with us.
   A: Thanks. I __________ (not eat) there yet, but I __________ (hear) it's pretty good.

B Look at things Matt said. Put the adverb in the correct place in the second sentence.

1. I'm very hungry. I haven't eaten ^yet. (yet)
2. I don't need any groceries. I've gone shopping. (already)
3. What have you done? Have you been to the zoo? (yet)
4. I called my parents before dinner. I've talked to them. (already)

2 Present perfect vs. simple past page 66

- Don't mention a specific time with the present perfect: I'**ve been** to a jazz club. Use the simple past to say when a past action happened: I **went** to a jazz club **last night**.

Complete the conversation using the present perfect or the simple past of the verbs in parentheses and short answers.

1. **A:** ___Did___ you ___see___ (see) the game last night? I really __________ (enjoy) it.
   B: Yes, I __________. It __________ (be) an amazing game. __________ you ever __________ (go) to a game?
   A: No, I __________. I __________ never __________ (be) to the stadium. But I'd love to go!
   B: Maybe we can go to a game next year.
2. **A:** __________ you ever __________ (be) to Franco's Restaurant?
   B: Yes, I __________. My friend and I __________ (eat) there last weekend. How about you?
   A: No, I __________. But I __________ (hear) it's very good.
   B: Oh, yes – it's excellent!

3 *For* and *since* page 67

- Use *for* + a period of time to describe how long a present condition has been true: We've been in New York **for two months**. (= We arrived two months ago.)
- Use *since* + a point in time to describe when a present condition started: We've been here **since August**. (= We've been here from August to now.)

Choose the correct word.

1. I bought my car almost 10 years ago. I've had it **for** / **since** almost 10 years.
2. The Carters moved to Seattle six months ago. They've lived there **for** / **since** six months.
3. I've wanted to see that movie **for** / **since** a long time. It's been in theaters **for** / **since** March.

UNIT 11

1 Adverbs before adjectives page 73

- Use *a/an* with (adverb) + adjective + singular noun: It's **a very modern city**. It's **an expensive city**. Don't use *a/an* with (adverb) + adjective: It's **really interesting**. (NOT: ~~It's a really interesting~~.)

Read the sentences. Add *a* or *an* where it's necessary to complete the sentences.

1. Brasília is ^an extremely modern city.
2. Seoul is very interesting place.
3. Santiago is pretty exciting city to visit.
4. Montreal is beautiful city, and it's fairly old.
5. London has really busy airport.

2 Conjunctions page 73

- Use *and* for additional information: The food is delicious, **and** it's not expensive.
- Use *but, though,* and *however* for contrasting information: The food is delicious, **but** it's very expensive./The food is delicious. It's expensive, **though/however**.

Choose the correct word.

1. Spring in my city is pretty nice, **and** / **but** it gets extremely hot in summer.
2. There are some great museums. They're always crowded, **and** / **however**.
3. There are a lot of interesting stores, **and** / **but** many of them aren't expensive.
4. There are many amazing restaurants, **and** / **but** some are closed in August.
5. My city is a great place to visit. Don't come in summer, **but** / **though**!

3 Modal verbs *can* and *should* page 75

- Use *can* to talk about things that are possible: Where **can** I get some nice souvenirs? Use *should* to suggest things that are good to do: You **should** try the local restaurants.
- Use the base form with *can* and *should* – not the infinitive: Where **can I get** some nice souvenirs? (NOT: ~~Where can I to get . . .?~~) **You should try** the local restaurants. (NOT: ~~You should to try . . .~~)

Complete the conversation with *can, can't, should,* or *shouldn't*.

A: I ___can't___ decide where to go on vacation. ________ I go to Costa Rica or Hawaii?
B: You ________ definitely visit Costa Rica.
A: Really? What can I see there?
B: Well, San Jose is an exciting city. You ________ miss the Museo del Oro. That's the gold museum, and you ________ see beautiful animals made of gold.
A: OK. What else ________ I do there?
B: Well, you ________ visit the museum on Mondays. It's closed then. But you ________ definitely visit the rain forest. It's amazing!

UNIT 12

1 Adjective + infinitive; noun + infinitive page 79

- In negative statements, *not* comes before the infinitive: With a cold, it's important **not to exercise** too hard. (NOT: ~~With a cold, it's important **to don't exercise** too hard~~.)

Rewrite the sentences using the words in parentheses. Add *not* when necessary.

1. For a bad headache, you should relax and close your eyes. (a good idea)
   It's a good idea to relax and close your eyes when you have a headache.
2. You should put some cold tea on that sunburn. (sometimes helpful)
   ______
3. For a backache, you should take some pain medicine. (important)
   ______
4. For a cough, you shouldn't drink milk. (important)
   ______
5. For a cold, you should take a hot bath. (sometimes helpful)
   ______
6. When you feel stressed, you shouldn't drink a lot of coffee. (a good idea)
   ______

2 Modal verbs *can, could,* and *may* for requests; suggestions page 81

- In requests, *can*, *could*, and *may* have the same meaning. *May* is a little more formal than *can* and *could*.

Number the lines of the conversation. Then write the conversation below.

____ Hi. Yes, please. What do you suggest for itchy skin?
____ Here you are. Can I help you with anything else?
____ Sure I can. You should see a dentist!
__1__ Hello. May I help you?
____ You should try this lotion.
____ Yes. Can you suggest something for a toothache?
____ OK. And could I have a bottle of pain medicine?

A: Hello. May I help you?
B: ______
A: ______
B: ______
A: ______
B: ______
A: ______

UNIT 13

1 *So, too, neither, either* page 87

- Use *so* or *too* after an affirmative statement: I'm crazy about sushi. **So** am I./I am, **too**.
- Use *neither* or *not either* after a negative statement: I don't like fast food. **Neither** do I./I don't **either**.
- With *so* and *neither*, the verb comes before the subject: **So am I**. (NOT: ~~So I am~~.) **Neither do I**. (NOT: ~~Neither I do~~.)

A Choose the correct response to show that B agrees with A.

1. **A:** I'm in the mood for something salty.
   B: I am, too. / I do, too.
2. **A:** I can't stand fast food.
   B: Neither do I. / I can't either.
3. **A:** I really like Korean food.
   B: So do I. / I am, too.
4. **A:** I don't eat French food very often.
   B: I do, too. / I don't either.
5. **A:** I'm not crazy about chocolate.
   B: I am, too. / Neither am I.

B Write responses to show agreement with these statements.

1. **A:** I'm not a very good cook.
   B: ______________________________
2. **A:** I love french fries.
   B: ______________________________
3. **A:** I can't eat very spicy food.
   B: ______________________________
4. **A:** I never eat bland food.
   B: ______________________________
5. **A:** I can make delicious desserts.
   B: ______________________________

2 Modal verbs *would* and *will* for requests page 89

- Don't confuse *like* and *would like*. *Would like* means "want."
- You can also use *I'll have* . . . when ordering in a restaurant to mean *I will have* . . .

Complete the conversation with *would, I'd,* or *I'll*.

A: ___Would___ you like to order now?
B: Yes, please. ____________ have the shrimp curry.
A: ____________ you like noodles or rice with that?
B: Hmm, ____________ have rice.
A: And ____________ you like a salad, too?
B: No, thanks.
A: ____________ you like anything else?
B: Yes, ____________ like a cup of green tea.

UNIT 14

1 Comparisons with adjectives page 93

- Use the comparative form (adjective + *-er* or *more* + adjective) to compare two people, places, or things: Which river is **longer**, the Nile or the Amazon? The Nile is **longer than** the Amazon. Use the superlative form (*the* + adjective + *-est* or *the most* + adjective) to compare three or more people, places, or things: Which river is **the longest**: the Nile, the Amazon, or the Mississippi? The Nile is **the longest** river in the world.
- You can use a comparative or superlative without repeating the noun: Which country is **larger**, Canada or China? Canada is **larger**. What's the highest waterfall in the world? Angel Falls is **the highest**.

Write questions with the words. Then look at the underlined words, and write the answers.

1. Which desert / dry / the Sahara or the Atacama?
   Q: *Which desert is drier, the Sahara or the Atacama?*
   A: *The Atacama is drier than the Sahara.*
2. Which island / large / Greenland, New Guinea, or Honshu?
   Q: ______
   A: ______
3. Which island / small / New Guinea or Honshu?
   Q: ______
   A: ______
4. Which U.S. city / large / Los Angeles, Chicago, or New York?
   Q: ______
   A: ______
5. Which ocean / deep / the Atlantic or the Pacific?
   Q: ______
   A: ______

2 Questions with *how* page 96

- Use *high* to describe mountains and waterfalls: How **high** is Mount Fuji? Angel Falls is 979 meters **high**. Use *tall* to describe buildings: How **tall** is the Empire State Building? (NOT: ~~How high is the Empire State Building?~~)

Complete the questions with the phrases in the box. There is one extra phrase.

How big	How cold	✓ How deep	How high	How tall

1. **Q:** *How deep* is Lake Baikal? **A:** It's 1,642 meters (5,387 feet) at its deepest point.
2. **Q:** ______ is Alaska? **A:** It's 1,717,900 square kilometers (663,300 square miles).
3. **Q:** ______ is Denali? **A:** It's 6,190 meters (20,310 feet) high.
4. **Q:** ______ is the Tokyo Skytree? **A:** It is 634 meters (2,080 feet) tall.

UNIT 15

1 Future with present continuous and *be going to*

page 101

- Use the present continuous to talk about something that is happening now: What **are** you **doing**? I'**m studying**. You can also use the present continuous with time expressions to talk about the future: What **are** you **doing tomorrow**? I'**m working.**
- Use *be going to* to talk about the future: I'**m going to** see an old school friend tomorrow.

A Read the sentences. Are they present or future? Write **P** or **F**.

1. Why are you wearing shorts? It's cold. ___P___
2. What are you wearing to the party on Friday? ________
3. What are you doing this weekend? ________
4. What are you doing? Can you please see who's at the door? ________
5. Are you going to see a movie tonight? ________

B Complete the conversations. Use *be going to*.

1. **A:** What ___are___ you and Tony going to ___do___ (do) tonight?
   B: We ____________ (try) the new Chinese restaurant. Do you want to come?
   A: I'd love to. What time ____________ you ____________ (go)?
   B: We ____________ (meet) at Tony's house at 7:00. And don't forget an umbrella. The weather forecast says it ____________ (rain) tonight.
2. **A:** Where ____________ you ____________ (go) on vacation this year?
   B: I ____________ (visit) my cousins in Paris. It ____________ (be) great!
   A: Well, I ____________ (not go) anywhere this year. I ____________ (stay) home.
   B: That's not so bad. Just think about all the money you ____________ (save)!

2 Messages with *tell* and *ask*

page 103

- In messages with a request, use the infinitive of the verb: Please ask her **to meet** me at noon. (NOT: ~~Please ask her meet me at noon~~.)
- In messages with negative infinitives, *not* goes before *to* in the infinitive: Could you ask him **not to be** late? (NOT: ~~Could you ask him to don't be late~~?)

Read the messages. Ask someone to pass them on. Use the words in parentheses.

1. Message: Patrick – We don't have class tomorrow. (please)
   Please tell Patrick that we don't have class tomorrow.
2. Message: Ana – Wait for me after class. (would)
   ____
3. Message: Alex – The concert on Saturday has been canceled. (would)
   ____
4. Message: Sarah – Don't forget to return the book to the library. (could)
   ____

UNIT 16

1 Describing changes page 107

- You can use several tenses to describe change – present tense, past tense, and present perfect.

A Complete the sentences with the information in the box. Use the present perfect of the verbs given.

buy a house	**change her hairstyle**	**join a gym**	**start looking for a new job**

1. Chris and Brittany ______________________________. Their apartment was too small.
2. Josh ______________________________. The one he has now is too stressful.
3. Shawna ______________________________. Everyone says it's more stylish.
4. Max ______________________________. He feels healthier now.

B Rewrite the sentences using the present tense and the words in parentheses.

1. Holly doesn't wear jeans anymore. *She wears dresses.* (dresses)
2. They don't live in the city anymore. ________________________ (in the suburbs)
3. Jackie isn't so shy anymore. ________________________ (more outgoing)
4. I don't eat greasy food anymore. ________________________ (healthier food)

2 Verb + infinitive page 109

- Use the infinitive after a verb to describe future plans or things you want to happen: I **want to learn** Spanish.

Complete the conversation with the verbs in parentheses in the correct form.

A: Hey, Zach. What *are you going to do* (go / do) after graduation?
B: Well, I ____________________ (plan / stay) here in the city for a few months.
A: Really? I ____________________ (want / go) home. I'm ready for my mom's cooking.
B: I understand that, but my boss says I can keep my job for the summer. So I ____________________ (want / work) a lot of hours because I ____________________ (hope / make) enough money for a new car.
A: But you don't need a car in the city.
B: I ____________________ (not plan / be) here for very long. In the fall, I ____________________ (go / drive) across the country. I really ____________________ (want / live) in California.
A: California? Where in California ____________________ (like / live)?
B: In Hollywood, of course. I ____________________ (go / be) a movie star!

Grammar plus answer key

Unit 1

1 Statements with *be*; possessive adjectives

1. This **is** Dulce Castelo**. She's** a new student from Santo Domingo.
2. My name **is** Sergio. **I'm** from Brazil.
3. My brother and I **are** students here. **Our** names are Nate and Chad.
4. **He's** Kento. **He's** 19 years old.
5. **They're** in my English class. **It's** a big class.

2 Wh-questions with *be*

2. e 3. a 4. b 5. c 6. d

3 Yes/No questions and short answers with *be*

1. A: Are they in your class?
   B: No, **they're not** / **they aren't**. They're in English 2.
2. A: Hi! **Are you** in this class?
   B: Yes, **I am**. I'm a new student here.
3. A: **Are you** from the United States?
   B: No, **we're not** / **we aren't**. We're from Calgary, Canada.
4. A: Hi, Monica. **Are you** free?
   B: No, **I'm not**. I'm on my way to class.
5. A: That's the new student. **Is he** from Paraguay?
   B: No, **he's not** / **he isn't**. He's from Uruguay.
6. A: **Is she** from Indonesia?
   B: Yes, **she is**. She's from Jakarta.

Unit 2

1 Simple present Wh-questions and statements

1. A: I **have** good news! Mona **has** a new job.
   B: How **does** she **like** it?
   A: She **loves** it. The hours are great.
   B: What time **does** she **start**?
   A: She **starts** at ten and **finishes** at four.
2. A: What **do** you **do**?
   B: I'm a teacher.
   A: What **do** you **teach**?
   B: I **teach** Spanish and English.
   A: Really? My sister **teaches** English, too.

2 Time expressions

B: I love it, but the hours are difficult. I start work **at** 6:30 A.M., and I work **until** 3:30.
A: That's interesting! I work the same hours, but I work **at** night. I start **at** 6:30 **in** the evening and finish **at** 3:30 **in** the morning.
B: Wow! What time do you get up?
A: Well, I get home **at** 4:30 and go to bed **at** 5:30. And I sleep **until** 2:00. But I only work **on** weekends, so it's OK. What about you?
B: Oh, I work **on** Monday, Wednesday, and Friday. And I get up **early** – around 5:00 A.M.

Unit 3

1 Demonstratives; *one, ones*

1. A: Excuse me. How much are **these** shoes?
   B: **They're** $279.
   A: And how much is **that** bag over there?
   B: **It's** only $129.
   A: And are the two gray **ones** $129, too?
   B: No. **Those** are only $119.
   A: Oh! **This** store is really expensive.
2. A: Can I help you?
   B: Yes, please. I really like **those** jeans over there. How much **are they**?
   A: Which **ones**? Do you mean **these**?
   B: No, the black **ones**.
   A: Let me look. Oh, **they're** $35.99.
   B: That's not bad. And how much is **this** sweater here?
   A: **It's** only $9.99.

2 Preferences; comparisons with adjectives

A

2. happier
3. more exciting
4. friendlier
5. more interesting
6. more reasonable
7. sadder
8. warmer

B

2. I like the silver one (better). It's more interesting.
3. I prefer the silk one. It's prettier.
4. I like the purple ones (more). They're cheaper.

Unit 4

1 Simple present questions; short answers

A

2. A: **Does John like** Carrie Underwood?
   B: No, **he doesn't**. John doesn't like country music.
3. A: **Does Lisa like** talk shows?
   B: Yes, **she does**. Lisa is a big fan of them.
4. A: **Do you / you and Kevin watch** the news on TV?
   B: Yes, **we do**. Kevin and I watch the news every night.
5. A: **Do you like** hip-hop?
   B: No, **I don't**. But I love R&B.
6. A: **Do your parents listen to** jazz?
   B: No, **they don't**. But my parents listen to a lot of classical music.

B

2. us 3. them 4. him 5. her

2 *Would*; verb + *to* + verb

A: Would you like to see a movie with me tonight?
B: Yes, I would. What would you like to see?
A: I'd like to see the new Matt Damon movie.

Unit 5

1 Present continuous

1. A: Really? **Is she living abroad?**
   B: Yes, **she is**. She**'s living** / **is living** in South Korea.
2. A: **How are you spending your summer?**
   B: **I'm working** part-time. I**'m taking** two classes also.
   A: **What are you taking?**
   B: My friend and I **are studying** photography and Japanese. We like our classes a lot.

2 Quantifiers

2. Nearly all students finish high school.
3. All children start school by the age of six.
4. A lot of couples have more than one child.
5. Few families have more than four children.

Unit 6

1 Adverbs of frequency

1. A: **I often play sports.**
2. Q: **Do you ever go jogging with a friend?**
   A: No, **I always jog / go jogging alone.**
3. Q: **How often do you play basketball?**
   A: I **play (basketball) four times a week.**
4. Q: **What do you usually do in the evening?**
   A: My family and I **almost always go online.**
5. Q: **How often do you go to the gym?**
   A: I **never go (to the gym).**

2 Questions with *how*; short answers

1. **How often** do you lift weights? c
2. **How well** do you play basketball? a
3. **How good** are you at volleyball? d
4. **How long** do you spend at the gym? b

Unit 7

1 Simple past

B: Yes, I **did**. I **had** a great time. My sister and I **went** shopping on Saturday. We **spent** all day at the mall.
A: **Did** you **buy** anything special?
B: I **bought** a new laptop. And I **got** some new clothes, too.
A: Lucky you! What clothes **did** you **buy**?
B: Well, I **needed** some new boots. I **got** some great ones at Great Times Department Store. What about you? What **did** you **do** on Saturday?
A: I **didn't do** anything special. I **stayed** home and **worked** around the house. Oh, but I **saw** a really good movie on TV. And then I **made** dinner with my mother. I actually **enjoyed** the day.

2 Past of *be*

2. He was at work all day.
3. Bruno and his co-workers were at work on Saturday, too.
4. They weren't at work on Sunday.
5. Was Bruno at home on Sunday?
6. Where was Bruno on Sunday?
7. He and his brother were at a baseball game.
8. They were at the park until 7:00.

Unit 8

1 *There is, there are; one, any, some*

1. A: **Are** there any supermarkets in this neighborhood?
   B: No, there **aren't**, but there are **some** on Main Street.
   A: And **is** there a post office near here?
   B: Yes, **there is**. It's across from the bank.
2. A: **Is** there a gas station around here?
   B: Yes, **there's** one behind the shopping center.
   A: Great! And are there **any** coffee shops nearby?
   B: Yes, there's a good **one** in the shopping center.

2 Quantifiers; *how many* and *how much*

A

1. A: Is there **much** traffic in your city?
   B: Well, there's a **little**.
2. A: Are there **many** Wi-Fi hotspots around here?
   B: No, there aren't **many**.
3. A: **How many** restaurants are there in your neighborhood?
   B: There **are** a lot.
4. A: **How much** noise **is** there in your city?
   B: There's **none**. It's very quiet

B

2. A: Are there many parks (in your neighborhood)?
3. A: Is there much crime (in your neighborhood)?
4. A: Are there many laundromats (in your neighborhood)?

Unit 9

1 Describing people

A: How tall is he?
B: He's 6 foot 2.
A: Does he wear glasses?
B: No, he doesn't. He wears contact lenses.
A: What color is his hair?
B: He has blond hair.
A: Does he have blue eyes?
B: No, he has brown eyes.
A: How old is he?
B: He's 26 – two years older than me.

2 Modifiers with participles and prepositions

1. B: She's the one wearing a red dress.
2. A: Which ones are your neighbors?
   B: They're the ones walking with the baby.
3. A: Which one is Jeff?
   B: He's the one with glasses.

Unit 10

1 Present perfect; *already, yet*

A

1. B: No, she **hasn't called** me, but I**'ve gotten** some emails from her.
2. A: **Have** you and Jan **had** lunch yet?
   B: No, we **haven't**. We're thinking of going to Tony's. **Have** you **tried** it yet? Come with us.
   A: Thanks. I **haven't eaten** there yet, but I**'ve heard** it's pretty good.

B

2. I've **already** gone shopping.
3. Have you been to the zoo **yet**?
4. I've **already** talked to them./I've talked to them **already**.

2 Present perfect vs. simple past

1. A: Did you see the game last night? I really **enjoyed** it.
   B: Yes, I **did**. It **was** an amazing game. **Have** you ever **gone** to a game?
   A: No, I **haven't**. I**'ve** never **been** to the stadium. But I'd love to go!
   B: Maybe we can go to a game next year.
2. A: **Have** you ever **been** to Franco's Restaurant?
   B: Yes, I **have**. My friend and I **ate** there last weekend. How about you?
   A: No, I **haven't**. But I**'ve heard** it's very good.
   B: Oh, yes – it's excellent!

3 *For* and *since*

1. I've had it **for** almost 10 years.
2. They've lived there **for** six months.
3. I've wanted to see that movie **for** a long time. It's been in theaters **since** March.

Unit 11

1 Adverbs before adjectives

2. Seoul is **a** very interesting place.
3. Santiago is **a** pretty exciting city to visit.
4. Montreal is **a** beautiful city, and it's fairly old.
5. London has **a** really busy airport.

2 Conjunctions

1. Spring in my city is pretty nice, **but** it gets extremely hot in summer.
2. There are some great museums. They're always crowded, **however**.
3. There are a lot of interesting stores, **and** many of them aren't expensive.
4. There are many amazing restaurants, **but** some are closed in August.
5. My city is a great place to visit. Don't come in summer, **though**!

3 Modal verbs *can* and *should*

A: I **can't** decide where to go on vacation. **Should** I go to Costa Rica or Hawaii?
B: You **should** definitely visit Costa Rica.
A: Really? What can I see there?
B: Well, San Jose is an exciting city. You **shouldn't** miss the Museo del Oro. That's the gold museum, and you **can** see beautiful animals made of gold.
A: OK. What else **can** / **should** I do there?
B: Well, you **can't** visit the museum on Mondays. It's closed then. But you **should** definitely visit the rain forest. It's amazing!

Unit 12

1 Adjective + infinitive; noun + infinitive

Possible answers:

2. For a sunburn, **it's sometimes helpful to put** some cold tea on it.
3. For a backache, **it's important to take** some pain medicine.
4. For a cough, **it's important not to drink** milk.
5. For a cold, **it's sometimes helpful to take** a hot bath.
6. When you feel stressed, **it's a good idea not to drink** a lot of coffee.

2 Modal verbs *can, could,* and *may* for requests; suggestions

2. Yes, please. What do you suggest for itchy skin?
3. You should try this lotion.
4. OK. And could I have a bottle of pain medicine?
5. Here you are. Can I help you with anything else?
6. Yes. Can you suggest something for a toothache?
7. Sure I can. You should see a dentist!

Unit 13

1 *So, too, neither, either*

A

2. B: I can't either.
3. B: So do I.
4. B: I don't either.
5. B: Neither am I.

B

1. B: I'm not either./Neither am I.
2. B: I do, too./So do I.
3. B: I can't either./Neither can I.
4. B: I don't either./Neither do I.
5. B: I can, too./So can I.

2 Modal verbs *would* and *will* for requests

B: I'll
A: Would
B: I'll
A: would
A: Would
B: I'd

Unit 14

1 Comparisons with adjectives

2. Q: Which island is the largest: Greenland, New Guinea, or Honshu?
   A: Greenland is the largest.
3. Q: Which island is smaller, New Guinea or Honshu?
   A: Honshu is smaller than New Guinea.
4. Q: Which U.S. city is the largest: Los Angeles, Chicago, or New York?
   A: New York is the largest.
5. Q: Which ocean is deeper, the Atlantic or the Pacific?
   A: The Pacific is deeper than the Atlantic.

2 Questions with *how*

2. How big
3. How high
4. How tall

Unit 15

1 Future with present continuous and *be going to*

A

2. F
3. F
4. P
5. F

B

1. B: We**'re going to try** the new Chinese restaurant. Do you want to come?
   A: I'd love to. What time **are** you **going to go**?
   B: We**'re going to meet** at Tony's house at 7:00. And don't forget an umbrella. The weather forecast says it**'s going to rain** tonight.
2. A: Where **are** you **going to go** on vacation this year?
   B: I**'m going to visit** my cousins in Paris. It**'s going to be** great!
   A: Well, I**'m not going to go** anywhere this year. I**'m going to stay** home.
   B: That's not so bad. Just think about all the money you**'re going to save**!

2 Messages with *tell* and *ask*

2. Would you ask Ana to wait for me after class?
3. Would you tell Alex (that) the concert on Saturday has been canceled?
4. Could you tell Sarah not to forget to return the book to the library?

Unit 16

1 Describing changes

A

1. Chris and Brittany **have bought a house**.
2. Josh **has started looking for a new job**.
3. Shawn **has changed her hairstyle**.
4. Max **has joined a gym**.

B

2. They live in the suburbs.
3. Jackie/She is more outgoing.
4. I eat healthier food now.

2 Verb + infinitive

B: Well, I **plan to stay** here in the city for a few months.
A: Really? I **want to go** home. I'm ready for my mom's cooking.
B: I understand that, but my boss says I can keep my job for the summer. So I **want to work** a lot of hours because I **hope to make** enough money for a new car.
A: But you don't need a car in the city.
B: I **don't plan to be** here for very long. In the fall, I**'m going to drive** across the country. I really **want to live** in California.
A: California? Where in California **would you like to live**?
B: In Hollywood, of course. I**'m going to be** a movie star!

Credits

The authors and publishers acknowledge the following sources of copyright material and are grateful for the permissions granted. While every effort has been made, it has not always been possible to identify the sources of all the material used, or to trace all copyright holders. If any omissions are brought to our notice, we will be happy to include the appropriate acknowledgements on reprinting and in the next update to the digital edition, as applicable.

Keys: E = Exercise; T = Top, B = Below, TR = Top Right, TL = Top Left, BR = Below Right, BL = Below Left, C = Centre, CR = Centre Right, CL = Centre Left, L = Left, R = Right, BC = Below Centre, B/G = Background.

Illustrations

337 Jon (KJA Artists): 17(T); **Mark Duffin**: 17(B), 80; **Thomas Girard** (Good Illustration): 50, 64, 66, 78(B), 108, 116–117; **Daniel Gray-Barnett**: 51, 57, 92; **Quino Marin** (The Organisation): 17(C), 18, 56, 70, 120; **Gavin Reece** (New Division): 2, 3, 5, 61, 123, 124; **Paul Williams** (Sylvie Poggio Artists): 60, 78(T).

Photos

Back cover (woman with whiteboard): Jenny Acheson/Stockbyte/GettyImages; Back cover (whiteboard): Nemida/GettyImages; Back cover (man using phone): Betsie Van Der Meer/Taxi/GettyImages; Back cover (woman smiling): PeopleImages.com/DigitalVision/GettyImages; Back cover (name tag): Tetra Images/GettyImages; Back cover (handshake): David Lees/Taxi/GettyImages; p. v: Caiaimage/Chris Ryan/GettyImages; p. 2 (header), p. vi (Unit 1): M G Therin Weise/Photographer's Choice RF/GettyImages; p. 4 (photo 1): Hill Street Studios/Tobin Rogers/Blend Images/GettyImages; p. 4 (photo 2): Steve Debenport/E+/GettyImages; p. 4 (photo 3): Monty Rakusen/Cultura/GettyImages; p. 4 (photo 4): Jose Luis Pelaez Inc/Blend Images/GettyImages; p. 4 (photo 5): Peter Cade/Iconica/GettyImages; p. 4 (photo 6): Sofia Bagdasarian/EyeEm/GettyImages; p. 4 (photo 7): Jon Feingersh/Blend Images/GettyImages; p. 4 (photo 8): Echo/Cultura/GettyImages; p. 6 (T): Caiaimage/Sam Edwards/Caiaimage/GettyImages; p. 6 (B): DragonImages/iStock/Getty Images Plus/GettyImages; p. 7 (T): Jamie McCarthy/Getty Images Entertainment/GettyImages; p. 7 (B): Pool/Samir Hussein/WireImage/GettyImages; p. 8 (header), p. vi (Unit 2): Hero Images/GettyImages; p. 8 (babysitter): Jonas unruh/E+/GettyImages; p. 8 (fitness instructor): Jutta Klee/Canopy/GettyImages; p. 8 (office assistant): Sturti/E+/GettyImages; p. 8 (sales associate): Matthias Tunger/DigitalVision/GettyImages; p. 8 (social media assistant): Tim Robberts/Taxi/GettyImages; p. 8 (tutor): Prasit photo/Moment/GettyImages; p. 9 (T): Hero Images/GettyImages; p. 9 (C): Westend61/GettyImages; p. 9 (B): Westend61/GettyImages; p. 10: Steve Debenport/E+/GettyImages; p. 11 (T): Marc Romanelli/Blend Images/GettyImages; p. 11 (B): Yellow Dog Productions/Iconica/GettyImages; p. 11 (taxi driver): Monty Rakusen/Cultura/GettyImages; p. 11 (Kristina): Yellow Dog Productions/Iconica/GettyImages; p. 13 (Danny): tulpahn/iStock/Getty Images Plus/GettyImages; p. 13 (Carla): Image Source/DigitalVision/GettyImages; p. 13 (Nico): Golero/E+/GettyImages; p. 13 (Lisa): Portishead1/E+/GettyImages; p. 14: Fabrice LEROUGE/ONOKY/GettyImages; p. 15 (engineer): B Busco/Photographer's Choice/GettyImages; p. 15 (caregiver): Maskot/GettyImages; p. 15 (electrician): Pamela Moore/E+/GettyImages; p. 15 (IT worker): Echo/Cultura/GettyImages; p. 15 (B): i love images/Cultura/GettyImages; p. 16 (header), p. vi (Unit 3): John Fedele/Blend Images/GettyImages; p. 16 (white mug): Steve Gorton/Dorling Kindersley/GettyImages; p. 16 (blue mug): Dorling Kindersley/GettyImages; p. 16 (green mug): Denis Gladkiy/iStock/Getty Images Plus/GettyImages; p. 16 (yellow mug): serggn/iStock/Getty Images Plus/GettyImages; p. 16 (orange mug): Markus Guhl/Stockbyte/GettyImages; p. 16 (red mug): ampols/iStock/Getty Images Plus/GettyImages; p. 16 (pink mug): Pavlo Vakhrushev/Hemera/Getty Images Plus/GettyImages; p. 16 (purple mug): Ozii45/iStock/Getty Images Plus/GettyImages; p. 16 (brown mug): spaxiax/iStock/Getty Images Plus/GettyImages; p. 16 (black mug): DaddyBit/iStock/Getty Images Plus/GettyImages; p. 16 (gray mug): ambassador806/iStock/Getty Images Plus/GettyImages; p. 17 (B): londoneye/E+/GettyImages; p. 17: Nick David/Iconica/GettyImages; p. 17: londoneye/Vetta/GettyImages; p. 19 (tie): Phil Cardamone/E+/GettyImages; p. 19 (bracelet): Elnur Amikishiyev/Hemera/Getty Images Plus/GettyImages; p. 19 (ring): frender/iStock/Getty Images Plus/GettyImages; p. 19 (shirt): gofotograf/iStock/Getty Images Plus/GettyImages; p. 19 (belt): clark_fang/iStock/Getty Images Plus/GettyImages; p. 19 (earrings): Tarzhanova/iStock/Getty Images Plus/GettyImages; p. 19 (flip flops): subjug/E+/GettyImages; p. 19 (socks): Gary Ombler/Dorling Kindersley/GettyImages; p. 19 (B): Klaus Vedfelt/Iconica/GettyImages; p. 20 (jacket): White Packert/The Image Bank/GettyImages; p. 20 (coat): Steve Gorton/Dorling Kindersley/GettyImages; p. 20 (orange sweater): ARSELA/iStock/Getty Images Plus/GettyImages; p. 20 (grey sweater): popovaphoto/iStock/Getty Images Plus/GettyImages; p. 20 (gold rings): Tarek El Sombati/E+/GettyImages; p. 20 (silver rings): Burazin/Photographer's Choice/GettyImages; p. 21 (TR): Ivo Peer/EyeEm/GettyImages; p. 21 (TL): martinedoucet/E+/GettyImages; p. 21 (BR): Richard Boll/Photographer's Choice/GettyImages; p. 21 (BL): Al Freni/The LIFE Images Collection/GettyImages; p. 22 (header), p. vi (Unit 4): Westend61/GettyImages; p. 22 (T): Philip Othberg/EyeEm/GettyImages; p. 23 (T): Mark Metcalfe/Getty Images Entertainment/GettyImages; p. 23 (C): Leon Bennett/WireImage/GettyImages; p. 23 (Seth): Halfpoint/iStock/Getty Images Plus/GettyImages; p. 23 (Leanne): Caiaimage/Martin Barraud/Caiaimage/GettyImages; p. 23 (B): Ollie Millington/WireImage/GettyImages; p. 24 (Adele): Joern Pollex/Getty Images Entertainment/GettyImages; p. 24 (Steph Curry): TPG/Getty Images Entertainment/GettyImages; p. 24 (Star Wars): Bravo/NBCUniversal/GettyImages; p. 24 (Top chef): Atlaspix/Alamy; p. 25 (Alexis): Todor Tsvetkov/E+/GettyImages; p. 25 (Jacob): Neustockimages/E+/GettyImages; p. 25 (Tyler): fotostorm/E+/GettyImages; p. 25 (Andrew): panic_attack/iStock/Getty Images Plus/GettyImages; p. 25 (B): Henrik Sorensen/Iconica/GettyImages; p. 25 (Connor): Hero Images/GettyImages; p. 25 (Camila): Tetra Images/Brand X Pictures/GettyImages; p. 27 (B): STAN HONDA/AFP/GettyImages; p. 27 (C): Noel Vasquez/GC Images/GettyImages; p. 27 (T): Michael Tran/FilmMagic/GettyImages; p. 28 (leather jacket): deniztuyel/iStock/Getty Images Plus/GettyImages; p. 28 (wool jacket): Leonid Nyshko/iStock/Getty Images Plus/GettyImages; p. 28 (silk shirt): popovaphoto/iStock/Getty Images Plus/GettyImages; p. 28 (cotton shirt): gofotograf/iStock/Getty Images Plus/GettyImages; p. 28 (laptop): MyImages_Micha/iStock/Getty Images Plus/GettyImages; p. 28 (desktop computer): Ryan McVay/Photodisc/GettyImages; p. 29: Chad Slattery/The Image Bank/GettyImages; p. 30 (header), p. vi (Unit 5): eli_asenova/E+/GettyImages; p. 30 (James): alvarez/E+/GettyImages; p. 30 (Betty): Image Source/GettyImages; p. 30 (Robert): Siri Stafford/Stone/GettyImages; p. 30 (Patricia): Courtney Keating/E+/GettyImages; p. 30 (Deborah): Juanmonino/E+/GettyImages; p. 30 (Arturo): Kevin Dodge/Blend Images/GettyImages; p. 30 (Joseph): Izabela Habur/E+/GettyImages; p. 30 (Keiko): Paul Simcock/Blend Images/GettyImages; p. 30 (Joshua): Liam Norris/Cultura/GettyImages; p. 30 (Nicole): Westend61/Brand X Pictures/GettyImages; p. 30 (Veronica): lukas_zb/iStock/Getty Images Plus/GettyImages; p. 30 (Andrew): BDLM/Cultura/GettyImages; p. 30 (Emily): Robert Daly/Caiaimage/GettyImages; p. 30 (Alyssa): Westend61/GettyImages; p. 30 (Ethan): Compassionate Eye Foundation/Photodisc/GettyImages; p. 31 (Quincy Jones): Jason LaVeris/FilmMagic/GettyImages; p. 31 (Rashida Jones): Barry King/FilmMagic/GettyImages; p. 31 (Ashton Kutcher): JB Lacroix/WireImage/GettyImages; p. 31 (Mila Kunis): Vera Anderson/WireImage/GettyImages; p. 31 (Emma Roberts): Noam Galai/Getty Images North America/GettyImages; p. 31 (Julia Roberts): Dan MacMedan/WireImage/GettyImages; p. 31 (Cameron Diaz): Jason LaVeris/FilmMagic/GettyImages; p. 31 (Nicole Richie): Jeffrey Mayer/WireImage/GettyImages; p. 31 (BL): Vladimir Serov/Blend Images/GettyImages; p. 31 (Max): Flashpop/DigitalVision/GettyImages; p. 31 (Tina): Michael Blann/Iconica/GettyImages; p. 31 (BR): Oliver Strewe/Lonely Planet Images/GettyImages; p. 32 (man calling): Jed Share/Kaoru Share/Blend Images/GettyImages; p. 32 (woman calling): Justin Lambert/DigitalVision/GettyImages; p. 32 (woman chatting): Johnny Greig/iStock/Getty Images Plus/GettyImages; p. 32 (girl chatting): Tim Robberts/The Image Bank/GettyImages; p. 33 (T): Stuart Fox/Gallo Images/GettyImages; p. 33 (B): David Sacks/DigitalVision/GettyImages; p. 33 (C): Aping Vision/STS/Photodisc/GettyImages; p. 33 (Luis): yellowdog/Image Source/GettyImages; p. 33 (Vicky): XiXinXing/GettyImages; p. 34 (T): Robert Daly/Caiaimage/GettyImages; p. 34 (B): Nerida McMurray Photography/DigitalVision/GettyImages; p. 35 (TR): Hero Images/GettyImages; p. 35 (TL): Francesco Ridolfi/Cultura/GettyImages; p. 35 (BR): Compassionate Eye Foundation/Natasha Alipour Faridani/DigitalVision/GettyImages; p. 35 (BL): Edgardo Contreras/Taxi/GettyImages; p. 36 (header), p. vi (Unit 6): Thomas Barwick/DigitalVision/GettyImages; p. 36 (TL): Thomas Barwick/Stone/GettyImages; p. 36 (TR): RuslanDashinsky/iStock/Getty Images Plus/GettyImages; p. 36 (swimming fins): Bluemoon Stock/Stockbyte/GettyImages; p. 36 (shoes): yasinguneysu/E+/GettyImages; p. 36 (golf ball): Duncan Babbage/E+/GettyImages; p. 36 (volley ball): pioneer111/iStock/Getty Images Plus/GettyImages; p. 36 (karate uniform): Comstock/Stockbyte/GettyImages; p. 36 (fitness ball): ayzek/iStock/Getty Images Plus/GettyImages; p. 36 (yoga mat): Serg Myshkovsky/E+/GettyImages; p. 36 (soccer ball): Creative Crop/DigitalVision/GettyImages; p. 36 (bicycle): Comstock/Stockbyte/GettyImages; p. 37 (TR): Mike Kemp/Blend Images/GettyImages; p. 37 (TL): Tim Kitchen/The Image Bank/GettyImages; p. 39 (TR): Jon Bradley/The Image Bank/GettyImages; p. 39 (BR): Studio J Inc/GettyImages; p. 39 (Steph): ATELIER CREATION PHOTO/iStock/Getty Images Plus/GettyImages; p. 39 (Mick): ATELIER CREATION PHOTO/iStock/Getty Images Plus/GettyImages; p. 40 (T): ImagesBazaar/GettyImages; p. 40 (Ex 12.1): Ann Summa/Photolibrary/GettyImages; p. 40 (Ex 12.2): Portra Images/Iconica/GettyImages; p. 40 (Ex 12.3): mediaphotos/E+/GettyImages; p. 40 (Ex 12.4): T.T/Stone/GettyImages; p. 41 (T): Maximilian Stock Ltd./The Image Bank/GettyImages; p. 41 (BR): Gary Burchell/DigitalVision/GettyImages; p. 42: Hero Images/GettyImages; p. 43: Diana Mulvihill/The Image Bank/GettyImages; p. 44 (header), p. vi (Unit 7): edwardolive/iStock/Getty Images Plus/GettyImages; p. 44 (social media): sturti/iStock/Getty Images Plus/GettyImages; p. 44 (go dancing): Tom Merton/Caiaimage/GettyImages; p. 44 (listen to music): Sam Edwards/Caiaimage/GettyImages; p. 44 (play video games): Robert Deutschman/DigitalVision/GettyImages; p. 44 (read): John Lund/Marc Romanelli/Blend Images/GettyImages; p. 44 (relax): SolStock/E+/GettyImages; p. 44 (spend time): Image Source/GettyImages; p. 44 (watch TV): Dan Dalton/Caiaimage/GettyImages; p. 44 (CR): Caiaimage/Paul Bradbury/OJO+/GettyImages; p. 44 (BR): Hero Images/GettyImages; p. 44 (Cara): Caiaimage/Paul Bradbury/OJO+/GettyImages; p. 44 (Neil): Ezra Bailey/Taxi/GettyImages; p. 45: Westend61/GettyImages; p. 46: chinaface/E+/GettyImages; p. 47 (T): AleksandarNakic/E+/GettyImages; p. 47 (B): Songquan Deng/iStock/Getty Images Plus/GettyImages; p. 48: Elena Elisseeva/iStock/Getty Images Plus/GettyImages; p. 49 (T): AYOTOGRAPHY/iStock/Getty Images Plus/GettyImages; p. 49 (C): Gato Desaparecido/Alamy; p. 49 (B): simon's photo/Moment/GettyImages; p. 50 (header), p. vi (Unit 8): GARDEL Bertrand/hemis.fr/GettyImages; p. 50: Miles Ertman/All Canada Photos/GettyImages; p. 52: Chris Bennett/GettyImages; p. 53 (downtown): Anne Sophie Dhainaut/EyeEm/GettyImages; p. 53 (suburb): Bob O'Connor/Stone/GettyImages; p. 53 (shopping district): Busà Photography/Moment/GettyImages; p. 53 (college campus): Witold Skrypczak/Lonely Planet Images/GettyImages; p. 53 (business district): Julian Elliott Photography/Photolibrary/GettyImages; p. 53 (theatre district): Jerry Driendl/Stone/GettyImages; p. 53 (industrial district): ULTRA.F/Taxi Japan/GettyImages; p. 53 (small town): Barry Winiker/Photolibrary/GettyImages; p. 53 (BR): UpperCut Images/Stockbyte/GettyImages; p. 53 (Alana): UpperCut Images/Stockbyte/GettyImages; p. 53 (Barry): franckreporter/E+/GettyImages; p. 54: Guillermo Murcia/Moment/GettyImages; p. 55 (T): Noriko Hayashi/Bloomberg/GettyImages; p. 55 (C): Alessandra Santorelli/REX/Shutterstock; p. 55 (B): migstock/Alamy; p. 58 (header), p. viii (Unit 9): Tom Merton/Caiaimage/GettyImages; p. 58 (long hair): Portra Images/DigitalVision/GettyImages; p. 58 (short hair): KidStock/Blend Images/GettyImages; p. 58 (straight hair): Rick Gomez/Blend Images/GettyImages; p. 58 (curly hair): Rainer Holz/Westend61/GettyImages; p. 58 (bald): wickedpix/iStock/Getty Images Plus/GettyImages; p. 58 (mustache and beard): shapecharge/E+/GettyImages; p. 58 (young): RedChopsticks/GettyImages; p. 58 (middle aged): Caiaimage/Chris Ryan/OJO+/GettyImages; p. 58 (elderly): David Sucsy/E+/GettyImages; p. 58 (handsome): Yuri_Arcurs/iStock/Getty Images Plus/GettyImages; p. 58 (good looking): Wavebreakmedia Ltd/Getty Images Plus/GettyImages; p. 58 (pretty): AntonioGuillem/iStock/Getty Images Plus/GettyImages; p. 58 (short): Ana Abejon/E+/GettyImages; p. 58 (fairly short): DRB Images, LLC/E+/GettyImages; p. 58 (medium height): 4x6/E+/GettyImages; p. 58 (pretty tall): momentimages/GettyImages; p. 58 (very tall): Photodisc/Stockbyte/GettyImages; p. 59: Tim Robberts/Taxi/GettyImages; p. 61 (Boho): Christian Vierig/WireImage/GettyImages; p. 61 (Classic): alekse/E+/GettyImages; p. 61 (Hipster): SeanShot/E+/GettyImages; p. 61 (Streetwear): Peter Muller/Cultura/GettyImages; p. 63 (TL): Robert Cornelius/Hulton Archive/GettyImages; p. 63 (BL): Dougal Waters/DigitalVision/GettyImages; p. 63 (TR): NASA/Getty Images North America/GettyImages; p. 63 (BR):

Tim Stewart News/REX/Shutterstock; p. 64 (header), p. viii (Unit 10): Paul Andrew Lawrence/Visuals Unlimited, Inc./GettyImages; p. 64 (theme park): Danielle Gali/AWL Images/GettyImages; p. 64 (go dancing): Diverse Images/UIG/GettyImages; p. 64 (space centre): Hiroyuki Matsumoto/Photographer's Choice/GettyImages; p. 64 (Cuban food): 424846/Hemera/Getty Images Plus/GettyImages; p. 64 (alligator): LaDora Sims/Moment/GettyImages; p. 67: Masaaki Toyoura/The Image Bank/ GettyImages; p. 68: Dan Dalton/Caiaimage/GettyImages; p. 69 (TR): Anna_Shepulova/ iStock/Getty Images Plus/GettyImages; p. 69 (CL): James Devaney/WireImage/ GettyImages; p. 69 (CR): Simon Brown NI/Photolibrary/GettyImages; p. 69 (BL): Romilly Lockyer/Photographer's Choice/GettyImages; p. 71: CoCam/iStock/Getty Images Plus/GettyImages; p. 72 (header), p. viii (Unit 11): Tetra Images/GettyImages; p. 72 (beautiful): Sylvain Sonnet/GettyImages; p. 72 (ugly): donvictorio/iStock/Getty Images Plus/GettyImages; p. 72 (BR): Jane Sweeney/AWL Images/GettyImages; p. 73: 2630ben/iStock/Getty Images Plus/GettyImages; p. 74 (CR): Andrew Bain/Lonely Planet Images/GettyImages; p. 74 (photo 1): Michele Falzone/The Image Bank/ GettyImages; p. 74 (photo 2): seng chye teo/Moment/GettyImages; p. 74 (photo 3): WitR/iStock/Getty Images Plus/GettyImages; p. 74 (photo 4): Photo by Hanneke Luijting/Moment/GettyImages; p. 74 (photo 5): f11photo/iStock/Getty Images Plus/ GettyImages; p. 74 (photo 6): Panoramic Images/Panoramic Images/GettyImages; p. 75 (TR): Julius Reque/Moment Mobile/GettyImages; p. 75 (CR): Christian Kober/ robertharding/GettyImages; p. 75 (Jason): svetikd/E+/GettyImages; p. 75 (Claudia): Hill Street Studios/Blend Images/GettyImages; p. 76 (TR): Eric Lo/Moment/ GettyImages; p. 76 (BR): 153photostudio/iStock/Getty Images Plus/GettyImages; p. 77 (TR): Manfred Gottschalk/Lonely Planet Images/GettyImages; p. 77 (CL): Jeremy Woodhouse/Photographer's Choice RF/GettyImages; p. 77 (CR): Kimberley Coole/ Lonely Planet Images/GettyImages; p. 78 (header), p. viii (Unit 12): Paul Bradbury/ Caiaimage/GettyImages; p. 79 (sore throat): BSIP/UIG/Universal Images Group/ GettyImages; p. 79 (fever): Tom Le Goff/DigitalVision/GettyImages; p. 79 (toothache): Eric Audras/ONOKY/GettyImages; p. 79 (burn): Jurgute/iStock/Getty Images Plus/ GettyImages; p. 80: annebaek/E+/GettyImages; p. 81 (TR): Yuri_Arcurs/E+/ GettyImages; p. 81 (BR): simarik/E+/GettyImages; p. 82: PeopleImages.com/ DigitalVision/GettyImages; p. 83: rbiedermann/iStock/Getty Images Plus/ GettyImages; p. 83 (B/G): Johnny Lye/iStock/Getty Images Plus/GettyImages; p. 85 (stomachache): IAN HOOTON/Science Photo Library/GettyImages; p. 85 (insect bite): BURGER/PHANIE/Canopy/GettyImages; p. 85 (nosebleed): LEA PATERSON/SCIENCE PHOTO LIBRARY/Science Photo Library/GettyImages; p. 85 (hiccups): Peopleimages/ iStock/Getty Images Plus/GettyImages; p. 85 (CL): Image Source/Photodisc/ GettyImages; p. 85 (C): Pascal Broze/ONOKY/GettyImages; p. 85 (CR): kali9/E+/ GettyImages; p. 86 (header), p. viii (Unit 13): Hero Images/Hero Images/GettyImages; p. 86 (apple pie): John Montana/StockFood Creative/GettyImages; p. 86 (chocolate): Thomas Francois/iStock/Getty Images Plus; p. 86 (french fries): Rachel Weill/UpperCut Images/GettyImages; p. 86 (hamburger): Westend61/GettyImages; p. 86 (icecream cone): Oksana Dzhaketi/EyeEm/EyeEm/GettyImages; p. 86 (pasta): jon whitaker/ Dorling Kindersley/GettyImages; p. 86 (sandwich): julie clancy/Moment/GettyImages; p. 86 (sushi): Foodcollection/GettyImages; p. 86 (BR): Cultura RM Exclusive/Matelly/ Cultura Exclusive; p. 87 (bland): powerbeephoto/iStock/Getty Images Plus/ GettyImages; p. 87 (delicious): Agnieszka Kirinicjanow/E+/GettyImages; p. 87 (greasy): Foodcollection/GettyImages; p. 87 (healthy): matka_Wariatka/iStock/Getty Images Plus/GettyImages; p. 87 (rich): Luzia Ellert/StockFood Creative/GettyImages; p. 87 (salty): magnetcreative/iStock/Getty Images Plus/GettyImages; p. 87 (spicy): Floortje/ E+/GettyImages; p. 88 (board): Jon Schulte/E+/GettyImages; p. 88 (B/G): Sonya_ illustration/iStock/Getty Images Plus; p. 88 (BR): andresr/E+/GettyImages; p. 89: NicoleArnoldPhotography/GettyImages; p. 90 (TR): Justin Geoffrey/Iconica/ GettyImages; p. 90 (girl): Peopleimages/E+/GettyImages; p. 90 (burger): Yurika Yamada/EyeEm/EyeEm/GettyImages; p. 91: JGI/Jamie Grill/Blend Images/ GettyImages; p. 92 (header), p. viii (Unit 14): Bjarki Reyr/Stone/GettyImages; p. 93: andresr/E+/GettyImages; p. 94 (L): Mint Images - Liesel Bockl/Mint Images RF/ GettyImages; p. 94 (C): Celia Peterson/arabianEye/GettyImages; p. 94 (R): Dave and Les Jacobs/Kolostock/Blend Images/GettyImages; p. 95 (T): Witold Skrypczak/Lonely Planet Images/GettyImages; p. 95 (B): Stuart Westmorland/Photographer's Choice/ GettyImages; p. 96: Al Rod/Stockbyte/GettyImages; p. 97 (TR): Canadian Space Agency/RADARSAT/NASA/Science Photo Library; p. 97 (CL): Australian Scenics/ Photolibrary/GettyImages; p. 97 (BR): TERADAT SANTIVIVUT/E+/GettyImages; p. 99: itkin_photo/iStock/Getty Images Plus/GettyImages; p. 100 (header), p. viii (Unit 15): Diverse Images/UIG/Universal Images Group/GettyImages; p. 100 (CR): Westend61/ GettyImages; p. 100 (BR): Hero Images/Hero Images/GettyImages; p. 102 (TR): Miroslav Georgijevic/Vetta/GettyImages; p. 102 (R): Ariel Skelley/Blend Images/ GettyImages; p. 102 (Jake): Ariel Skelley/Blend Images/GettyImages; p. 102 (Caitlin): Joan Vicent Canto Roig/E+/GettyImages; p. 103: Robert Daly/Caiaimage/ GettyImages; p. 105 (TR): Todor Tsvetkov/E+/GettyImages; p. 105 (CL): Tony Garcia/ Image Source/GettyImages; p. 105 (CR): Getty Images/Staff/Getty Images News/ GettyImages; p. 105 (BL): Cultura Exclusive/We Boldly Went/Cultura Exclusive/ GettyImages; p. 106 (header), p. viii (Unit 16): AndreyPopov/iStock/Getty Images Plus/ GettyImages; p. 106 (BR): Westend61/GettyImages; p. 107 (TR): franckreporter/E+/ GettyImages; p. 107 (CR): Yagi Studio/DigitalVision/GettyImages; p. 107 (BR): Catherine Delahaye/Taxi/GettyImages; p. 109 (CR): Peopleimages/E+/GettyImages; p. 109 (BR): Caiaimage/Tom Merton/OJO+/GettyImages; p. 110 (TR): andresr/E+/ GettyImages; p. 110 (CR): andresr/E+/GettyImages; p. 111 (TR): Michel Porro/Getty Images News/GettyImages; p. 111 (B): REMKO DE WAAL/Stringer/AFP/GettyImages; p. 112: Aksonov/Vetta/GettyImages; p. 113: Wavebreakmedia Ltd/Wavebreak Media/ Getty Images Plus/GettyImages; p. 114 (TL): wdstock/iStock/Getty Images Plus/ GettyImages; p. 114 (BL): wdstock/iStock/Getty Images Plus/GettyImages; p. 114 (R): Hero Images/GettyImages; p. 115 (CL): Rachel Watson/The Image Bank/GettyImages; p. 115 (CR): GMVozd/E+/GettyImages; p. 115 (BL): Zero Creatives/Cultura/ GettyImages; p. 115 (BC): Rosiane Goncalves/EyeEm/GettyImages; p. 115 (BR): Stuart O'Sullivan/Stone/GettyImages; p. 116 (TL): loops7/E+/GettyImages; p. 116 (TR): Richard Boll/Photographer's Choice/GettyImages; p. 116 (CL): Thomas Northcut/ Photodisc/GettyImages; p. 116 (CR): makkayak/E+/GettyImages; p. 117 (TL): Hemera Technologies/PhotoObjects.net/Getty Images Plus/GettyImages; p. 117 (TR): by_ nicholas/iStock/Getty Images Plus/GettyImages; p. 117 (BL): imagenavi/GettyImages; p. 117 (BR): dandanian/E+/GettyImages; p. 118 (bike riding): Phillip Suddick/Taxi/ GettyImages; p. 118 (street fair): Hill Street Studios/Blend Images/GettyImages; p. 118 (dancing): Morsa Images/Iconica/GettyImages; p. 118 (laundry): AndreyPopov/ iStock/Getty Images Plus/GettyImages; p. 118 (clean house): Alin Dragulin/Vico Collective/GettyImages; p. 119 (learning language): Westend61/GettyImages; p. 119 (raising child): kupicoo/E+/GettyImages; p. 119 (renovating house): Tetra Images/ GettyImages; p. 119 (working in country): A. Chederros/ONKYO/GettyImages; p. 119 (writing blog): Hero Images/GettyImages; p. 119 (driving car): Weekend Images Inc./ E+/GettyImages; p. 119 (going college): Clerkenwell/Vetta/GettyImages; p. 119 (travelling): JGI/Jamie Grill/Blend Images/GettyImages; p. 119 (playing band): moodboard/Cultura/GettyImages; p. 119 (singing choir): Erik Isakson/Tetra Images/ Brand X Pictures/GettyImages; p. 119 (question mark): pearleye/E+/GettyImages; p. 121 (noodles): Keiko Ikeda/EyeEm/GettyImages; p. 121 (soccer ball): Wolfgang Weinhaeupl/GettyImages; p. 121 (hotel): Trinette Reed/Blend Images/GettyImages; p. 121 (cake): Stefanie Sudek/STOCK4B-RF/GettyImages; p. 121 (museum): De Agostini/A. Dagli Orti/De Agostini Picture Library/GettyImages; p. 121 (smartphone): Grassetto/iStock/Getty Images Plus/GettyImages; p. 122 (airport): Westend61/ GettyImages; p. 122 (bank): Alina Vincent Photography, LLC/E+/GettyImages; p. 122 (bookstore): Paolo Cordelli/Lonely Planet Images/GettyImages; p. 122 (café): Luis Alvarez/Taxi/GettyImages; p. 122 (clothing store): Betsie Van Der Meer/Taxi/ GettyImages; p. 122 (drugstore): Tom Merton/OJO Images/GettyImages; p. 122 (grocery store): 97/E+/GettyImages; p. 122 (gym): Hero Images/GettyImages; p. 122 (hair salon): Peathegee Inc/Blend Images/GettyImages; p. 122 (hospital): Caiaimage/ Robert Daly/OJO+/GettyImages; p. 122 (movie theatre): dolgachov/ iStock/Getty Images Plus/GettyImages; p. 122 (newsstand): Andrew Hetherington/Stone/ GettyImages; p. 122 (outdoor market): Hero Images/GettyImages; p. 122 (park): Janusz Ziob/Moment/GettyImages; p. 122 (shopping mall): Michael H/DigitalVision/ GettyImages; p. 122 (stadium): Simon Bruty/The Image Bank/GettyImages; p. 126 (TR): Erik Von Weber/Taxi/GettyImages; p. 126 (CR): Christian Kober/Photographer's Choice/GettyImages; p. 126 (CL): Inti St Clair/Blend Images/GettyImages; p. 127 (hiccups): Jupiterimages/Photolibrary/GettyImages; p. 127 (yawning): JGI/Jamie Grill/ Blend Images/GettyImages; p. 127 (stressed): BSIP/UIG/Universal Images Group/ GettyImages; p. 127 (mosquito bite): art-4-art/E+/GettyImages; p. 127 (sneezing): Compassionate Eye Foundation/David Oxberry/OJO Images Ltd/DigitalVision/ GettyImages; p. 128: Hero Images/Hero Images/GettyImages; p. 129 (Kaua'i): M Swiet Productions/Moment/GettyImages; p. 129 (Manaus): Marcelo Andre/Photolibrary/ GettyImages; p. 129 (B/G): © HO Soo Khim/Moment/GettyImages; p. 130 (L): JGI/ Jamie Grill/Blend Images/GettyImages; p. 130 (CR): Hero Images/Hero Images/ GettyImages; p. 130 (BR): Garry Wade/Taxi/GettyImages; p. 131 (CR): Jessica Peterson/GettyImages; p. 131 (TR): Nasser Mar/ EyeEm/GettyImages.